The Intimate Connection

By James B. Nelson
published by The Westminster Press

*The Intimate Connection: Male Sexuality,
Masculine Spirituality*

Moral Nexus: Ethics of Christian Identity and Community

Other books by James B. Nelson

The Responsible Christian

Human Medicine: Ethical Perspectives on New Medical Issues

Rediscovering the Person in Medical Care

Embodiment: An Approach to Sexuality and Christian Theology

*Between Two Gardens: Reflections on Sexuality
and Religious Experience*

Human Medicine: Revised and Expanded Edition
(with Jo Anne Smith Rohricht)

The Intimate Connection

Male Sexuality, Masculine Spirituality

James B. Nelson

The Westminster Press
Philadelphia

Scripture quotations from the Revised Standard Version of the Bible are copyrighted 1946, 1952, © 1971, 1973 by the Division of Christian Education of the National Council of the Churches of Christ in the U.S.A. and are used by permission.

Grateful acknowledgment is made for excerpts from the following copyrighted material:

W. H. Auden, lines from "For the Time Being," reprinted by permission of the publisher, Random House, Inc., from *W. H. Auden: Collected Poems,* edited by Edward Mendelson, copyright © 1976 by Edward Mendelson, William Meredith and Monroe K. Spears, executors of the Estate of W. H. Auden.

Dietrich Bonhoeffer, lines from "Who Am I?", from *Letters and Papers from Prison,* enlarged edition, edited by Eberhard Bethge, copyright © 1953, 1967, 1971 by SCM Press, Ltd. Reprinted with permission of SCM Press, Ltd., and Macmillan Publishing Company.

James Kavanaugh, "Of Liberation," from *Maybe If I Loved You More* (New York: E. P. Dutton, 1982), copyright © 1982 by James Kavanaugh. Reprinted with permission of the author.

Book design by Gene Harris

First edition

Published by The Westminster Press ®
Philadelphia, Pennsylvania

PRINTED IN THE UNITED STATES OF AMERICA

9 8 7 6 5

Library of Congress Cataloging-in-Publication Data

Nelson, James B., 1930–
   The intimate connection.

   1. Men—United States.   2. Masculinity (Psychology)
3. Spirituality—United States.   I. Title.
HQ1090.3.N44   1988   305.3'1   87-29487
ISBN 0-664-24065-8

Contents

Preface   7

ONE   Male Sexuality and Masculine Spirituality   11

TWO   Embracing Sexual Mystery   29

THREE   Embracing Friendship   47

FOUR   Embracing Mortality   67

FIVE   Embracing Masculinity   85

SIX   New Ways in Our Sexual Spirituality   113

Notes   133

Preface

During my wrestling with the issues of this book, I was reminded again and again that we are indeed "surrounded by a great cloud of witnesses," a cloud that includes many fellow searchers. A number of groups extended gracious invitations, which provided occasions for presenting earlier versions of some of this material. The dialogues that arose in those settings enriched me greatly, and I want to acknowledge my gratitude. The groups, listed alphabetically, were these: The American Association of Pastoral Counselors; Grace Episcopal Cathedral, San Francisco (The Eastburn Lectures); Kirk-ridge Retreat Center; Naramata Retreat Center; The New England Pastors' School (United Church of Christ); Northern Illinois Conference of the United Methodist Church; Pacific School of Religion; Princeton Theological Seminary; The Protestant Episcopal Seminary of Virginia; The Riverside Church, New York; Rocky Mountain Conference of the United Methodist Church; and the University of the Pacific (The Colliver Lectures). Certain elements of two chapters also appeared in *The Christian Century* and *SIECUS Report.*

In addition, my sincere thanks go to a number of persons who are reflected in these pages in ways they may not recognize (but which I would gladly point out, should they ask): my brother members of a support group we fondly call "The Manly Men"—Jim Boen, James Frank Mossman, Bill Seabloom, Jim Siefkes, and Wilson Yates; treasured colleagues at United Theological Seminary of the Twin Cities, importantly including members of elective courses in Men's Liberation and Spirituality; and good friends at a distance who have shared these concerns—Bob Blaney, Jim Dittes, Jim Lehmann, Merle Longwood, David Maitland, and Bob Raines. Finally, my appreciation goes to David Long-Higgins for valuable manuscript assistance.

The Intimate Connection

ONE

Male Sexuality
and Masculine Spirituality

"All real American men love to fight."
—General George S. Patton

"My friends have no friends. . . . The reason for that is that we are all men—and men, I have come to believe, cannot or will not have real friends."
—Richard Cohen, *Washington Post* columnist

"All I knew was that you had to run, run, run, without knowing why you were running."
—Allan Sillitoe in *The Loneliness of the Long Distance Runner*

"[The possibility of the 'wildman' is] the possibility that the deep, nourishing and spiritually radiant energy in the male lies not in the feminine side, but in the deep masculine. . . . Now that so many men are getting in touch with their feminine side, we're ready to start seeing the wildman and to put his powerful, dark energy to use."
—Robert Bly, poet

All the above statements, however different from each other, have something in common. Whether their authors intended it or not, all are speaking of the links between male sexuality and masculine spirituality. We are setting out to explore some of those connections.

The exploration is important. During the past two decades, feminist women have been actively searching out the relationships between their sexualities and their spiritualities. Their discoveries have been illuminating—indeed, exciting. They have found that what they have experienced *as women* and *as female* is of enormous significance in understanding their relationships to God, the world, others, and themselves. We who are men are starting to realize that the same is true for us, but our quest is only beginning.

We have been slow because we, especially those of us who are white and economically secure, are the privileged caste in a male-dominated society. Those in the seats of power usually take their perceptions of the world for granted, accepting their own experiences as normative. But the time is overdue for our own exploration, for our own reassessment, and for our own fresh learnings.

We know it is overdue when we hurt. Male sexual health is not a particularly bright picture at the present time. What are some of the current facts?[1] Though more male babies are born each year in our society (106 to 100 females), fewer males survive past the first six months. During the first year of life the male death rate is one third higher than that of females. Part of the reason may well be the different ways in which baby boys are treated. Some research suggests, for example, that the greater susceptibility of males to sudden infant death syndrome (SIDS) is because boys have less touch and physical nurture early in life.

The large majority of boys born in America are circumcised within three days of birth. This still occurs even though the national organizations of obstetricians and pediatricians have long questioned the medical necessity of routine circumcision. It is a procedure typically done without anesthetic, and one that causes more pain to the infant than is often acknowledged. Further, incidences of infection, hemorrhage, and surgical trauma are considerably higher than is usually recognized. Nor do we know how to assess the emotional trauma.

Early childhood is a crucial time for the development of positive self-understandings. Current evidence is clear, however, that boys are slower in developing positive body images than are girls, that boys are less secure about their gender roles, and that boys tend to cling to rigid and stereotypical concepts of masculinity. The pressures against "effeminacy" and its dreaded suggestion of homosexuality are particularly strong in adolescence, but actually begin much earlier.

We often think that adolescent boys are more comfortable with their sexuality than are girls of that age. True, they typically begin sexual experimentation earlier. In particular, they masturbate sooner and more frequently. Yet peer pressure tells them that this is second-class sexual behavior and they really ought to "make it" with girls. Thus begins precocious sexual activity, with boys typically assuming little responsibility for birth control. A large percentage of teenage boys are intoxicated during their first sexual experiences; that fact, plus the press toward "virility" to prove that one is straight, is not a good recipe for contraception planning. While traditional role expectations assume that boys are sexually knowledgeable and initiators, all available studies show that from adolescence through adulthood males possess less accurate information about sexual matters than do females.

Nor, on the whole, do we who are adult males show impressive signs of sexual health. At latest count, we die about seven years earlier than do women. In the narrowly sexual arena, we are typically ignorant about the prevention and early detection of testicular and prostatic cancers, yet these are among the leading cancer threats for men. Our incidences of suicide, chemical dependency, penal incarceration, and violent death are vastly higher than are women's. Pressures toward "masculinity" appear to keep us away from counselors, psychotherapists, and physicians much longer, but when we finally submit to serious illness we are hospitalized 15 percent longer than women for the same condition. Our difficulty in expressing emotions is directly linked with the higher incidence of major diseases. Indeed, of the ten leading causes of death, it appears that only one (diabetes) is not significantly associated with the masculine role.[2]

It is not a very encouraging picture. We are hurting. But the hurting goes beyond the physical. It is found in our yearning for emotional intimacy with other males—sons, fathers, and friends— yet finding ourselves unprepared, unequipped, and fearful of that intimacy. The hurt is in our wanting relationships of genuine equality and mutuality with women, yet finding ourselves crippled by centuries of male sexism and by our emotional dependencies on the opposite sex. The hurt is in our discovery that we have bought heavily into the message that our self-worth is directly dependent upon our occupational success, and yet the idol of work somehow does not deliver its promised salvation.

But the hurting also goes far beyond the personal and interpersonal realms. If being men according to the patterns we have been taught can be dangerous to our own health, it can be at least as dangerous to the health of others and to the planet itself. True, the enormous social problems we face on a world scale in violence, racism, poverty, human rights, and environmental abuse are all extraordinarily complicated in their causes. However, each of them has important connections with distorted expressions of masculinism. Some of the connections are obvious and direct; some are subtle and indirect. But they are unmistakably there.

I suspect that men who read books such as this are, as I am, not only hurting but also deeply yearning. We are yearning for closer, more fulfilling, more life-giving connectedness with others, with our world, and with ourselves. This means we are yearning for closer

connectedness with God, the heart of the universe itself. When we
yearn for life-giving relationships with any person or part of creation,
we are at the very same time reaching for God. For, according to an
incarnationalist faith, God is the spiritual presence who becomes
incarnate in and through creaturely flesh. Another way of saying this
is that we are simply longing for more life-giving connectedness
between our sexuality and our spirituality.

As fundamental as all of this is, I suspect we have another yearning
that is very real for us: we simply want to feel genuinely good about
being men. But sometimes that seems complicated.

On the one hand, we did not choose to be born male, nor can we
accept responsibility for all the damage and injustice caused by male
sexism, past and present. We do not wish to feel constantly guilty
about that which we did not intend and did not do. We were born
male, and most of us would not choose to be anything else. We enjoy
being male.

On the other hand, we have absorbed some of the feminist critique
of patriarchy and of our own stubborn sexism. We are aware of some
of the destructive aspects of the traditional male role—historically,
in others, and, indeed, in ourselves. Furthermore, when we are both
sensitive and honest, we are aware of two other things. One, we know
that the sin of sexism continues in some insidious ways within us, as
much as we have tried to be liberated from it. We have not recovered.
Rather, we are "recovering sexists." It is a lifelong process. Further,
we know that, even though we are trying to rid ourselves of the
destructive aspects of a distorted masculinism, and even when we
earnestly strive for a more healed and just human existence, we still
reap daily benefits from being male in a still-patriarchal world. We
earn more money for the same work; power and position come to us
more readily.

So this healing reunion of our sexuality and our spirituality is not
a simple thing. But any steps on the way, however painful, can be
enormously worthwhile and enormously exciting.

Some Personal Comments and Perspectives

This book is a piece of a personal journey. The external facts about
me are rather unremarkable: white, middle-class, middle-aged, married, professional spouse, two grown and married children, theological seminary professor, payer on home mortgage, and so on. Our
social locations always condition our perspectives. The reader ought
to know where the writer is coming from in order to make the
necessary course corrections.

At least as important as those quite ordinary life circumstances,

I believe, is that I have written this because I feel deeply and personally involved in the questions. And I believe in André Maurois's perspective on this matter. He maintained that the need to express oneself in writing usually springs from unresolved inner conflicts. The writer does not write because of having found answers to the problem, but instead from having discovered the problem and wanting solutions. And the solution is not really a resolution so much as a deeper consciousness of the issue, coming from having wrestled with the problem.[3]

So I write as a man trying to understand who he is, who he has been, who he is becoming. And as one trying to understand what the world is like because of men, and what it might yet be. It is a journey with many companions who have been my teachers and mutual supporters, my challengers and confronters. Many unnamed men have furnished insights for these pages—members of my men's support group, other male friends and professional colleagues, numerous men with whom I have touched lives in retreats and workshops, and, significantly, my son. Many women are on these pages, especially feminist women and especially my wife and daughter. Gay men and lesbians, including numerous good friends, have taught me an enormous amount about men's issues. So also have people in Central America, people in peace movements, people with AIDS, people struggling for a faithful Christian church. Men's issues are everywhere, affect everyone, and need hosts of experiential vantage points to illumine them.

In spite of all of these teachers, this book comes out of a limited base of experience, and it has a limited focus. As is already evident, I write out of a white, middle-class, North American, and Christian perspective. I believe that some of the concerns to follow will apply equally to men of color and men of other ethnic, economic, religious, and geographical situations. Obviously, other things will not apply. Several examples of differences are in order:

Before the physical and cultural invasion of the whites, many American Indian tribes defined gender by social role rather than by a person's biological sex. They created a third gender, the "berdache," a man who did not conform to the standard male role. Often homosexually oriented, the berdache dressed differently and had different social functions. He was not seen as a deviant, however; in fact, he was honored because of his special spiritual powers. Gender flexibility still characterizes some non-urban Indian life, as a Lakota shaman explains: "To us, a man is what nature, or his dreams, make him. We accept him for what he wants to be."[4]

Middle-class fathers generally view themselves as role models, hoping that their sons will find their lives worthy of emulation. It is not necessarily so in working-class families. In *Working,* Studs Terkel reports these words from an interview: "If you ever wind up in that steel mill like me, I'm gonna hit you right over the head. Don't be foolish. Get yourself a schooling. Stay out of the steel mill or you'll wind up the same way I did."[5] Two other students of social class say this: "To call the pressure working-class fathers put on their kids 'authoritarian' is misleading in that the father doesn't ask the child to take the parents' lives as a model but as a warning."[6]

American black men's patterns of masculinity inevitably reflect their need to cope with a racist society. They often resist the glib condemnation of all macho behavior and assert that certain behaviors on their part can be powerful assertions of pride and identity in the face of white racism.[7]

Historically, Jewish men in America have had a standard of masculinity different from the dominant white pattern. Their traditional emphasis on literacy and love of learning has not fit the traditional American male mold. Further, Jewish men have been characterized as being emotional, nurturing, and caring. One says, "Jewish men hug and kiss, cry and laugh. A little too much. A little too loudly."[8]

Some things in this book will apply to men such as those represented above. Other things will not. I recognize that, and it is simply the reality of the limits of my experience and understanding. What about gay males? Again, some accents in gay experience will not be reflected here simply because I have not had them. However, I suspect that gays who share my general life situation in other respects will find that a great deal of our male sexual-spiritual experience is held in common.

The focus of this book is limited in another way, as the title suggests: male sexuality and masculine spirituality. Soon I will try to define what I mean by those terms. I do use them broadly. However, "broadly" does not mean that all major areas of men's lives are examined. For example, much more could be developed on certain topics such as work and male life stages. But excellent books recently have brought theological reflection to bear on these issues.[9] Furthermore, my accent is on sexual dynamics, with a particular attention to male *body* life. I have chosen issues I think might usefully illustrate that focus.

"Body theology," thus, is a major perspective informing my approach. In Christian terms, it is "incarnational theology." Unfortunately, most theologizing throughout Christian history has not taken seriously the reality that when we reflect theologically, we do so as embodied selves. The ancient dualistic split between spirit and body (or mind and matter) and its companion split between man and woman continue to wreak their havoc. Male theologians, in particular, have long assumed that the arena of theology is that of spirit and mind, far removed from the inferior, suspect body. So most theology has begun more deductively than inductively. It has started with propositions and abstractions and then attempted to move from the abstract to the concrete. It has begun with universals and then moved to particulars.

Incarnational or body theology starts the other way around. It moves from the particular outward toward the more inclusive. It begins with the concrete. Elie Wiesel provides one illustration. He knows that he must start with the particularity of the Jew, not universal humanity. But that does not lock him into exclusively Jewish concerns: "By struggling on behalf of Russian, Arab, or Polish Jews, I fight for human rights everywhere. By calling for peace in the Middle East, I take a stand against every aggression, every war. . . . Only by drawing on his unique Jewish experience can the Jew help others. A Jew fulfills his role as man only from inside his Jewishness."[10] In fact, a universal perspective is a fiction. That is the fault of so much male-written theology over the centuries: it assumed that it was speaking universally, when in fact it was speaking out of a particular male experience.

Body theology begins with the concrete. It does not begin with broad doctrinal formulations about God and humanity. Rather, it begins with the bodily experiences of life: making breakfast and making love; beef burgundy and bloated bellies of starving children; daily calendars and deadly carcinomas; missives we pen to those we love and missiles we aim at those we fear. It begins with the many big and little birthings and dyings we encounter daily.

Male body theology begins with the concreteness that men experience as men. This does not mean we cannot make any generalizations about men. What it does mean is that we must try to look at our human experience with the consciousness that we are interpreting it from a *male's* experiential viewpoint. We have no Olympian vantage point from which to stand above our sexual place. What we see is what we see as certain kinds of men from certain kinds of social situations. What we perceive we perceive from within male bodies whose biology is not a universal human biology.

It is precisely such particularity that makes studies of men's experience so needed. About ten years ago I first offered a seminary elective course on theology and men's liberation. I was initially surprised by the indignation of some women students when the course was first announced. Their point: women effectively had been written out of male-biased theology for all these centuries with the result that virtually everything except explicitly feminist studies was in fact "male theology." Why a special course on men and theology now? Isn't 99 percent of Christian theology already "male theology"? It was an understandable objection I should have anticipated, even though my intent was quite other than to perpetuate the patterns of the past.

The feminist critique of traditional male scholarship and male theology is right: women *have* been written out, and the result is that these materials simply do not adequately reflect women's experiences. But something else has happened as well. When we have assumed the stance of "generic man," the stance in which male lives are presumed to be the norm for *human* lives, we have not only lost understanding of women's experience, we have also lost knowledge of men's experience insofar as it is specifically *men's.* Because traditional scholarship and theology made men into pseudo-universal generic human beings, it excluded from consideration whatever was specific to men *as men.* Our task, then, is to try to understand the experiences of masculinity as specific male phenomena rather than as phenomena assumed to be universally human.

The consequences of this approach should be good for us all, women as well as men. By this approach we can tap into men's seldom-examined body experiences as male. We can explore the subterranean male fears that go with the territory of being masculine. We can also make masculinity visible as particular and specific and deprive generic "man" of its hegemony on truth. We can become sensitized to the strident masculinism of Andrew Jackson in combat with the Indians and of Theodore Roosevelt in his "bully little wars." We can become aware of the particular male experiences that have shaped so many Christian understandings of God, human nature, sin, grace, love, power, and justice. All of us should benefit.

Men and Masculinity: Where Are We Moving?

The current time is not the first era in our society in which there has been concern about the meanings of masculinity.[11] The issue was a powerful one late in the nineteenth century, the time during which our contemporary understandings of gender roles were significantly shaped. Only in the last fifteen years of that century did the words "heterosexual" and "homosexual" begin to find their way into common use. During roughly the same period the closing of the frontier, changes in the nature of work following rapid industrialization, and the apparent "feminization" of American culture through the women's suffrage movement and women's increasing dominance in the socializing milieu of home, Sunday school, and school led to anxieties about masculinity. Thus, it was not surprising that in the first years of the twentieth century manuals were published counseling young men on the perils of femininity, and the Boy Scouts of America and the YMCA were founded as conscious attempts to reverse the tides eroding manhood.

The last years of the twentieth century show some parallels. The frontiers of American influence abroad are waning. The second major wave of American feminism has come with force. A visible gay culture has arisen. There are fears for a nation grown indolent, losing out in international competition, and going "soft" on communism. A radical right wing in both religion and politics sets its primary agenda around "traditional values," which centrally means a return to traditional masculinity.

Yet some changes are occurring in the male gender stereotype in our society. Traditionally, males have been expected to be physically strong, instrumental, goal-oriented, focusing on achievement, lacking in emotional and interpersonal skills, and relating to women in a dominant manner. The changing version, at least among younger middle-class men, places more emphasis on intellectual than physical strength, more on interpersonal skills and companion-style relations with women. But some parts of the stereotype seem highly resistant to change: work is still seen as the primary criterion of a man's worth and self-esteem, and men's emotional expressiveness is still very restricted.[12]

Because of feminist questions and changes, but also because of the strains men have been feeling in their male roles, many men in the past two decades have begun to reevaluate their lives, and a men's liberation movement has slowly arisen. For the most part, the movement has not been driven primarily by a passion to change the social system, for men still perceive themselves deriving too many benefits from the system as it is. Instead, the focus has been more heavily upon personal confusions and stress, and the seeking of other men's support. The movement is small but growing; its signs are support groups, conferences, newsletters, journals, and books. The movement is diverse. A considerable part is explicitly pro-feminist and supportive of gay men. Another wing focuses on divorce reform, angered by the impact of divorce settlements on men. Still others are of the "no-guilt" orientation, the philosophy that men as well as women are victims of gender roles and men have no reason to feel guilty in relation to women. And the groups overlap.

While many in this movement are men of the church, specifically

Christian and theological dimensions of men's reassessment and change have been slow to appear. But they are now coming. Some local church men's groups that used to specialize in pancake breakfasts and movies of the last World Series have shifted to serious study and the sharing of men's lives in biblical-Christian perspective. National church men's gatherings now show the impact of the men's quest for different identities. And now, belatedly, we are even beginning to write down some theological reflections about these things.

Regarding Sex and Gender

Language is always important. It is both a key to our understandings of reality and a shaper of those understandings. So some clarity about our words is crucial at this point.

As it applies to the differences between males and females, *sex* is a biological term. People are either female or male depending on their sex organs and genes. *Gender* is a psychological and social term. It refers to our subjective feelings of maleness or femaleness (gender identity) and to the social evaluation of our behaviors as masculine or feminine (gender role). *Sex role,* likewise, refers to social expectations that are applied to persons of a given biological sex.[13]

I will try to use the words carefully in the above ways. The distinctions are important. They remind us that our basic identities and behaviors are not simply *determined* by our biology. Indeed, the important work of John Money and colleagues has shown that persons born with ambiguous sex organs or organs that do not correspond to their genetic sex find their gender identity primarily through the social influences of parents and others close to them early in life.[14] Thus, even sex differentiation is not entirely simple.

After birth, most physical differences between the two sexes are ones of degree, not kind, and the observable differences depend upon complex *interactions* of nature and nurture, biology and social influences. This applies to physical size, physiological processes, particular mental functions, vulnerability to disease, and activity levels. Many differences among men themselves and many differences among women themselves are greater than those between the two sexes. The only clear sex differences culture cannot change are that women can menstruate, gestate, and lactate while men cannot; men can impregnate, while women cannot.[15]

Later I will speak of men's distinctively male bodily experience. I believe this is an important reality—as is women's distinctively female body experience for them. To overlook this is to fall into another expression of sexual dualism, a belief that the body plays no significant role in our lives and that all is determined by mind or spirit as influenced by society. But everything I say about our body experiences should be understood in light of the above affirmations: that there is no sharp absolute dualism between the two sexes, and that the meanings of our male and female body lives are the result of complex biological and social interactions.

This is the difference between the recognition of *dualities* in our sexual experience, on the one hand, and the assumption of *dualism* on the other. Too frequently we move subtly from the first to the second, from recognition of relative differences to assumptions about superiority and inferiority. Beverly Wildung Harrison says it well: "I believe we must begin by rejecting the notion that there is any *fundamental* dimorphism in human nature/being. . . . If there are statistically significant psychological or physiological differences between men and women, the moral question is, 'What are we to make of these differences in human history and society?' No conceivable biological or psychological differences can justify gender-based distinctions in social power, prestige, and wealth."[16]

Thus we will be walking a fine line in what is to come. On the one hand, the psychosocial elaborations of male biological sex are enormously plastic and malleable, as is true for female biological sex. Further, having a male body is never an excuse for oppressive behavior. On the other hand, there are distinctive experiences that boys and men have *precisely because of* their male bodies. The same is true for girls and women because of their own female biology. While these body-grounded experiences never fully *determine* one's spiritual contours, they do exercise considerable *influence*. And these intimate body-spirit connections deserve more exploration than they have yet received.

Spirituality

In the most general sense, by spirituality I mean the ways and patterns by which the person—intellectually, emotionally, and physically—relates to that which is ultimately real and worthful for him or her. This, admittedly, is a broad definition. Spirituality has not always been so understood.

In the first millennium of Christianity the understanding of spirituality was profoundly influenced by dualistic perceptions. I have already alluded to dualism, but it deserves more elaboration. Dualism is any radical splitting apart of things that essentially belong together. Under the impact of late Hellenistic Greek philosophy and culture, the early church was deeply influenced by *spiritualistic dualism,* the notion that the "spirit" (sometimes called the "mind" or the "soul") was essentially different from and superior to the "body" (or "matter"). While this notion was scarcely present in the Hebrew understanding (the Old Testament typically speaks of the unitary nature of human selfhood), it did make its inroads into the Christian church. Spirit came to be understood as the eternal and good part of the self, while the body was mortal, temporal, subject to decay and death. Furthermore, since sexuality seemed to be such a body phenomenon, it was most often viewed with deep suspicion as the chief source and vehicle of sin.

If the Hebraic culture was largely free from the spirit-body split, it was hardly free from the other side of sexual dualism's coin: patriarchy. Here was *sexist dualism*, the systematic subordination of women to men. It was women's subordination in interpersonal relations, in every social institution, and in the culture's fundamental ways of perceiving and experiencing the world and God. The Old Testament admittedly does contain passages which challenge patriarchy, passages in which sexual mutuality is celebrated. Further, female imagery is occasionally used in reference to God. Nevertheless, patriarchy dominates the Old Testament pages. God is characterized primarily through masculine images and language. Women are viewed as property, valued for their role in procreation but effectively disenfranchised by Israelite religious law. And it was men most often who were believed to bear *nepesh*, or spirit, and thus able to function as spokespersons for Yahweh's own breath and power.

The dawning of the Christian era saw both continuities and differences. Accounts of the Christian gospel contained strong unitary, antidualistic elements. With the Hebrew scriptures, the church also proclaimed a theology of the created goodness of all being. In addition the early church voiced the startling proclamation of God's incarnation in human flesh. Further, some portions of Christian scripture contained the vision of the radical equality of all persons ("neither Jew nor Greek . . . neither male nor female"). Even so, the two forms of sexual dualism frequently won the day, and, indeed, they often coalesced into one powerful composite dualism. Males came to identify themselves essentially with spirit and mind, while at the same time they identified females with body and matter. And in any dualism there is a clearly understood hierarchy: the "higher" must control the "lower."

Thus a powerful pyramid of control was erected. God (who was "pure spirit" and perceived in largely masculine images) must control all of creation. Within creation, men (whose spirits and minds must control their own bodies and emotions) must control women (who are more bodily and emotional, deficient in reason). Adults must control children (who are less spiritual and rational in their undeveloped states). Human beings must control the soulless animals, while animals are superior to plants and plants to inorganic nature.

This worldview of dualistic divisions and hierarchical controls, though contrary to the core of the gospel, deeply affected the church. One consequence was a certain perception of Christian spirituality, which came to dominate the church for many centuries. It was a life controlled by disciplines of prayer and meditation whereby one was enabled to rise to higher, often mystical, communion with God. Popular piety typically understood this as involving the mysterious activity of "spiritual techniques" designed for the purification and focusing of "the interior life" of the soul. Its only connections with bodily and sexual life were those of discipline (sometimes "mortification") of this lower realm. Such spirituality still persists for many Christians. Holiness is tantamount to bodilessness, and saints are sexless people, mystically attuned to a life transcending earthly matter. This spirituality became a sure recipe for individualistic pietism, because it blinded its adherents to the recognition that material well-being and justice are intrinsically part of spiritual blessedness.

After the Reformation of the sixteenth century, differences in Roman Catholic and Protestant spirituality began to emerge. The Catholic tradition had accented the individual's own effort toward union with God, union involving both purgation and illumination. The Protestant mode now emphasized the joyful experience of gracious forgiveness, leading to sanctification. The sanctity or holiness toward which one was enabled to grow was not so much a process of following deliberate rules and special spiritual practices under the supervision of a priestly director, but now more the devotional and moral disciplines that one accepted for the living of all of life.

While the differences between Catholic and Protestant spiritualities can be unfairly exaggerated, they were there. But two things remained common to both. One was that proper spirituality and the means thereto were generally defined by the *male* church leadership. The second, not surprisingly, was that spiritual holiness was largely disconnected from body and flesh. Indeed, the idea that Christian spirituality might involve the celebration of one's flesh, the affirmation and healing of one's sexuality, and an earthy, sensuous passion toward life was largely foreign.

There were exceptions. Significantly, these nondualistic exceptions were largely expressed by women, and women had been taught that they were essentially bodily. The few men who voiced these things were quite promptly branded as heretics. These exceptions came largely from the Catholic medieval tradition. Hildegard of Bingen (1098–1179), a monastery abbess, physician, and artist, wrote: "Holy

persons draw to themselves all that is earthly. . . . The earth is at the
same time mother. She is the mother of all that is natural, mother
of all that is human." Dame Julian of Norwich (1342–1415), a nun
who embraced an earthy spirituality, said, "Our sensuality is
grounded in Nature, in Compassion, and in Grace. In our sensuality,
God is. God is the means whereby our Substance and our Sensuality
are kept together so as never to be apart." Mechthild of Magdeburg
(1210–1280), an unmarried laywoman who became a nun late in life,
expressed the spiritual connection clearly: "Do not disdain your
body. For the soul is just as safe in its body as in the Kingdom of
Heaven."[17]

Spirituality in the first and broadest sense, then, is a neutral term.
It can be good or bad, creative or destructive, dualistic or holistic,
or quite a mix. It is simply *our basic life orientations and the patterned
ways in which we express them.* It is the patterning of our thinking,
feeling, experiencing, and nurturing of whatever we take to be fundamentally important. It can be body-rejecting or body-affirming. But
everyone has, at any given point in life, a spiritual shape.

Christian spirituality, that patterning of life around those experiences of God in the faith community centered in Christ, is a fearful
mix of things. Historically, it has often been deeply distorted by the
sexual dualisms that divorce spirit from body, mind from matter,
reason from emotion, men from women, people from the rest of
nature, and heaven from earth. But there have also been other voices
and practices of far greater promise, as we have seen. They have held
out the possibility of our connectedness. So, whether we think of
spirituality in general or of Christian varieties in particular, in this
first sense of the term, spirituality simply means whatever shapes our
lives take toward the objects of our ultimate trust.

In another (perhaps surprising) sense of the word, spirituality is
the embracing of the life of the flesh. Christian theology and piety too
often have misunderstood Paul's contrasts between the "life of the
spirit" and "life of the flesh." Too frequently we have interpreted
these phrases as unvarnished dualism, as if Paul were simply exalting
the good eternal spirit over against the corruptible and corrupting
physical-sexual body. Now it is true that Paul was not always consistent. Some parts of his thought do hint at Greek dualism. But on
this particular score he has been ill-treated. Actually, he does not
usually mean sensuality by "the mind of the flesh *(sarx)*" but typically uses the term to denote our alienated attempts to save ourselves
by our own works. Nor does he mean an anti-body spiritualism by
"the mind of the spirit," but rather that life organized around our
acceptance of God's gracious acceptance of us.[18]

John S. Dunne's distinction between life in the flesh and life in the spirit is compatible with Paul's best intents.[19] By "flesh" Dunne means our histories composed of passing things and events. By "spirit" he refers to our *positive relationship* to those histories. Life in faith (spirituality in this positive sense) means embracing our own fleshly histories, not abandoning or denying them. Such spirituality is in contrast to those popular pieties which are highly selective about life in the flesh, choosing those attitudes and behaviors which seem to flatter the self and avoiding those which are ambiguous and give us discomfort. Popular spirituality is frequently more like Paul's "life in the flesh"—an attempt to ignore our shadows and distortions and, instead, to believe in our own self-righteousness. But such spirituality is self-defeating. Dunne puts it this way: "God becomes God in the moment when man becomes man."[20] (Though he is using the generic sense of "man," Dunne's sentence might apply in a particular way to those of us who are male.)

David S. Maitland expands on this same theme: "God becomes the living God . . . only as we are able to consent to those parts in our story of which we have become conscious. Prior to our awareness of the hopelessly mixed character of our individual stories we really only feign belief in God. . . . Our so-called belief in God was really either an intellectual assertion unconnected to our experience or an expression of self-satisfaction uninformed by self-acquaintance."[21]

Knowing and consenting to our lives, as Maitland maintains, is neither approving of everything we have been and done nor is it blindness to our need for forgiveness. Rather, it is honesty. It is the opposite of avoidance, concealment, and pretense. Though we tend to avoid it, "the difficult work of self-acquaintance" is necessary. Some of us who believe we are saved by divine grace might be tempted to think that self-knowledge is unnecessary. And those of us who rely on our own self-proving efforts to achieve our worth will be tempted to give "selective inattention" to aspects of our own stories. But precisely when we embrace our own fleshly histories as *our* stories, warts and all, then our healing becomes possible. Maitland concludes, "That gift [our healing] is surely from God and is not the consequence of our efforts. Rather, it is a gift of grace, a gift which frees the believer to *undertake* the hard work."[22]

This book is about our male journeys into such spirituality. It is about knowing and embracing our male sexual stories in their joys *and* in their pains, in their creativity *and* in their destructiveness. It is an attempt to be honest about our ambiguities as men, that we might celebrate those things wherein we have been life-giving and open ourselves to the gracious energies of healing where we have been life-denying.

Sexuality

And what about our sexuality? It includes sex and gender, but it is far more. Biological sex itself is gradually determined long before our conscious awareness, and in the latter part of fetal development there appear to be sexual feelings. Intrauterine photography has now produced pictures of male erection and female vaginal lubrication in fetuses. Regardless of age or physical condition, whether "sexually active" or celibate, we are all sexual beings until death. For our sexuality is far more than genital activity. It is our way of being in the world as gendered persons, having male or female biological structures and socially internalized self-understandings of those meanings to us. Sexuality means having feelings and attitudes about being "body-selves." It means having affectional orientations toward the opposite sex, the same sex, or quite possibly toward both. It means having the capacity for sensuousness.

Above all, sexuality is the desire for intimacy and communion, both emotionally and physically. It is the physiological and psychological grounding of our capacity to love. At its undistorted best, our sexuality is that basic *eros* of our humanness—urging, pulling, luring, driving us out of loneliness into communion, out of stagnation into creativity. Indeed, the word "sexuality" itself comes from the Latin *secare,* meaning "to cut or divide." The word suggests our appetite for a wholeness that can be appeased only through intimacy. It suggests the primitive human longing for reunion and communion. Sexuality thus is a deep human energy driving us toward bonding and compassion, and without it life would be cold and metallic. Even in its distorted and destructive expressions, sexuality betrays this fundamental longing. It is God-given for no less than that.[23]

Yet our sexuality is shaped not only by personal experiences and desires but also by the interests and requirements of social institutions. For example, Augustine was a primary theological shaper of the procreative norm as central to sexuality's meaning. But we need to understand his thought in the historical-social context of threat to the family. Maternal and infant mortality was exceedingly high, the economic and political structures were based on kinship, and the family seemed to be the only dependable social unit in a time of civil wars and barbarian invasions. Likewise, clerical celibacy was in part shaped by the economic interests of the church: single male clergy would not produce offspring who in turn would fight over church property. So also the prohibitions against homosexuality were in part grounded in the interests of a male church hierarchy in preserving its rational ordering unaffected by the passions of personal-sexual ties. And the anti-pleasure climate of Victorian sexuality in part was shaped by the need of the Industrial Revolution for a public morality of hard work, dedication, and delayed gratification. When we remember and understand such examples of sexuality's deep historical and social nature, we also remember how dynamic and susceptible to change it is. For those of us interested in some new ways of sexual spirituality, that is assuring.

The intimate connection of sexuality and spirituality is thus our hope and our exploration. More particularly, we are concerned about *male* sexuality and *masculine* spirituality. The two words are a bit tricky, and our dictionaries do not fully resolve the issue. Regarding *male*, dictionaries typically give first of all a biological definition: that sex which has an X and Y chromosome pair and normally also a penis, scrotum, and testicles. So far that seems clear enough. It is simply a biological category. In their second definitions under this entry, however, dictionaries usually speak of "male" as those characteristics suitable for human individuals of this sex, with examples such as "masculine" and "virile." Now social definitions have been layered onto biological ones, and the distinction between "male" and "masculine" is becoming fuzzier.

Regarding *masculine*, the dictionaries usually speak of those qualities which are deemed characteristic of or suitable to human males, such as vigor, strength, manliness, and boldness. At least this word is clear: it refers to social and cultural meanings and not essentially biology. However, there is ambiguity here as well. Both the "is" and the "ought to be" are present in these descriptions, both the descriptive and the normative. Not only are the definers talking about the qualities which *actually* seem to characterize human males but also those which are believed suitable to them, those qualities males *ought* to have.

My use of the words will not escape ambiguity. *Male* sexuality surely has a biological reference. I am convinced that the male sexual bodies which men have—indeed, which men *are*—do encourage certain kinds of experiences and perceptions that are not simply culturally defined. Because of our biology, we who are men do have certain tendencies and inclinations in life experience. The same is true of women because of their bodies. However, to speak of "tendencies and inclinations" is not to argue for a biological determinism. Our sexuality is at least as much a matter of our social creations as it is of our biologies, and perhaps even more so. Thus I will try to give due attention to *both* dimensions of male sexuality: that dimension boys and men have by virtue of their biology, and those meanings boys and men are taught to believe as appropriate for males.

In exploring *masculine* spirituality, I am interested in both those qualities seen characteristic of men and those believed suitable to men. Both the "is" and the "ought to be" deserve our attention. "Characteristic of" is descriptive. We need to understand how we ourselves and men in general tend to express spirituality. "Suitable to" goes beyond the descriptive to the normative: beyond telling how it is, to speaking of how we want it to be. What ought our masculine spirituality look like if we who are men might experience greater healing and wholeness? And if we might contribute more fully to the healing and wholeness of the earth?

TWO
Embracing
Sexual Mystery

The apparently endless quest for new information on lovemaking techniques and the latest secrets of sexual arousal testify that something is missing or wrong. In a society ostensibly so open and permissive about sexual matters, this might seem surprising. Yet all of us, male and female, have internalized dualistic messages that make our sexual expression far more complicated than the sex manuals portray. Some are confusing double messages: "Sex is God-given and beautiful, but don't talk about it, especially in church." Or the double message most of us acquired in our youth: "Sex is dirty; save it for someone you love."

Men, however, typically encounter a range of specific problems. These are some of those frequently observed:

Men are goal-oriented in sex; it is the orgasm that counts.

Men bring to the sex act numerous concerns about their technical performance: Did I do well? Did I satisfy my partner?

Men believe they must be in charge; they feel responsible for orchestrating the lovemaking and feel responsible for its "success."

Men have difficulty communicating their own desires and limits.

Men have an unusual concern for living up to their images of "normal" male sexual functioning and are terrified by the thought of "not being a real man."

Men have difficulty reading accurately their own emotional feelings about sex.

Men are uncomfortable with prolonged sensual play.

Men believe that all intimate physical contact should lead to genital sex, and that they should always want it and be ready for it. And they have a right to it.[1]

These, of course, are generalizations. Surely not all of them fit all men. Some of them fit heterosexuals more than gays. But many of them fit most men at least some of the time. While genital sex is only one mode of sexual expression, and while for some men—those who are celibate—it is not a chosen mode, these problems in men's love-making provide a window on deeper issues in male sexuality. Let us look in some detail at three of those underlying issues, probing their connections with men's spirituality. The three are sexism, genitaliza-tion, and separation.

Sexism: Dynamics and Costs

Most straight men and some gays are uncomfortable unless they take charge during intercourse, at least most of the time. The modes of being in charge may well be thoughtful, subtle, tender—initiating with loving strategies, feeling responsible for the partner's orgasm, restraining one's own satisfaction until it is clear that the occasion will be a success. Or the ways of being in charge can be more obvious: the missionary position, man on top, is the "right" way. Or the take-charge ways can be blatant: sex is a man's right, and the partner should know that. And in the midst of all this, in the most intimate of human moments, we have difficulty knowing what we are feeling. As in intercourse, so in life generally.

If sexist dualism, man over woman, affects our lovemaking, it also affects every other aspect of our personal and public lives. It is a major mark of male sexuality. Its costs are enormous, and women bear the brunt. It is they who have been forced into derivative identities, they who continue to experience subjugation in countless interpersonal and institutional forms, they who have been taught that they do not own their own bodies. What men have suffered, and still do, in fairness simply cannot be equated. That is the first thing we must say, and say it clearly and honestly.

Having voiced that, we can also honestly say that we men have been hurt also. We have lost touch with a whole range of emotions— we simply don't *feel* very well. We are more alienated from our bodies. We tend to lose touch with the concreteness of life, becoming seduced by abstractions and confusing them with reality. We live much of the time needing to prove ourselves through achievement and triumph. We relate competitively, especially with other men, and find vulnerability frightening. We die too soon. We have imaged the divine in masculine ways and then have found God distant. Our social institutions become skewed and frequently violent in ways clearly related to patriarchal patterns. We have created a hierarchy of control of nature that threatens our global ecology and survival.

How did it all happen? And why is it so difficult to change, both personally and institutionally?

Anthropologists tell us it has not always been this way.[2] Matrilineal and matrifocal societies seem to have predated patriarchies. Some societies developed sacred power-symbol systems which imaged the divine largely in female terms. This typically happened when the natural and social environments were friendly—when weather was not harsh, food was abundant, and other groups were largely congenial. Sacred power then appeared evident in the abundance of creation. Since women were most connected to the reproductive functions, and birthing seemed particularly connected with divine power, they were free to tap into that sacred permission to be powerful.

In other cases, the environments were not as friendly. The harshness and unpredictability of weather, the scarcity of food, and the hostility of neighboring groups all conspired to give the feeling that divine power was needed to ward off enemies of all kinds. Physical survival was paramount, and often had to be attained through dangerous hunting, trickery, or battle. Prolonged and helpless human infancy, together with the requirements of many pregnancies under harsh survival conditions, kept women from such activities. Men were more expendable, hence the more dangerous economic functions became theirs. When that happened, sacred power was imaged in masculine terms and sanctioned male social dominance. (It should give us pause that this sanctioning of male power apparently came not because of an initial belief in men's superiority but rather because of their expendability.)

The societies in unfriendly environments apparently were more numerous, and men's success in hunting and warfare led to their becoming the lawmakers, the religious leaders, and the cultural definers of social beliefs. Male puberty rites developed, which took the pubescent boy out of the female world of his early socialization and identified him with the male community. Now he had to win the title of being "a man" through rites of passage involving painful, often violent, ordeals—circumcision, fasting, beatings, the killing of enemies or wild animals. During these experiences the elders taught the boy that manhood meant bravery, armoring oneself against attack, and being able to suffer in silence without complaint. He learned that manhood involved the systematic control, domination, even destruction of the tender and vulnerable elements within himself.

At the same time the female childbearing and child-rearing roles became separated from the adult male world. Parallel communities with complementary functions emerged. The woman's world was birthing, early child nurture, cooking, and making clothing and domestic implements. Girls went through their puberty initiations as introductions on an adult level back into a world from which they had never been divorced, that of the mother. But the boy had to enter a strange new world. It was laced with fearful stories of how women had once controlled culture but how those original matriarchies had been overthrown by men. The man's world was both strenuous and privileged. Manhood had to be earned and maintained in the midst of danger. It was also a world of the elite, where men possessed the more highly valued cultural activities of special ritual and leisure functions. Man's world seemed to transcend the lower sphere of daily necessity. Woman's world was one of nature, body, and necessity, a lower realm that threatened to drag men down and restrict their freedom.

The split between male/ divine and female/nature was much more pronounced in certain cultures than in others. Babylonian and Canaanite mythology saw the divine much more within rather than transcendent to the natural world, both in its powers of chaos and in its renewal. Divinity, nature, and the female powers were combined. In Hebrew and Greek mythology, the worlds of our own heritage, however, the picture was different. In Hebrew thought, God was above nature, shaping it as an artisan shaped an object. Natural chaos was an instrument of divine wrath, and nature that which needed to be redeemed. In Greek thought, even more dramatically, the dualism was radically present. Male consciousness was closely identified with the transcendent status of the divine, outside of and above nature. The world of nature, matter, body, and woman was an inferior realm needing subjugation and control.

Such inheritance has contributed mightily to the shaping of our sexualities. I did not grow up knowing any of this anthropology or history. Nor did I know of the ways in which my own Christian religious heritage reflected patriarchal perceptions. But I did not really need to know of the misogyny of Tertullian or Thomas Aquinas or Luther or Calvin. It was in the air I breathed, and that was enough. So I grew up knowing that men had the particular responsibility and destiny to rule and control—nature, body, and women.

The long patriarchal inheritance both expressed and was compounded by biological misinformation. Aquinas, the chief theologian of the Middle Ages, took into his thought many perceptions of Aristotle, not the least of which was the dominance of male over female. To both thinkers, the female was "a defective male." Nature intended male babies, but when the father's powers were low or the weather was wrong, females resulted. But they were ontologically inferior, signified by the fact that the female fetus received its soul much later than did the male. Further, for most of recorded history, common belief has held that the male semen alone was the bearer of life. Women were the earth into which the seed was planted. Women were the incubators of the life transmitted by men. Indeed, not until the early nineteenth century did western science discover the details of the female reproductive process. Nor did I know any of this historical detail as my sexual perceptions were being shaped. Somehow, though, I did get the notion, both from my father and from the Boy Scouts, that my male sexual fluid was never to be "wasted" outside of marriage. It was precious and life-bearing.

History's confusions are compounded by psychology. Freud had an elaborate theory of castration anxiety as a common male experience. The engulfing of the male organ by the female in intercourse could lead unconsciously to anxiety about its loss. Men coped with this anxiety, he believed, by transforming it into aggression against the female. I am not sure how common castration anxiety is in men, but there is a related consciousness that I believe is pervasive: performance anxiety. For "successful" heterosexual intercourse, I must perform—have an erection, be potent. Impotence is a man's threat, always waiting in the wings while he is onstage. But whether sexual impotence has ever been a problem or not, the potency/impotency syndrome becomes symbolic of life itself for one conditioned in the masculine mode. The performance mode of life is always demanding, and failure always lurks in the shadows. Because it is a strenuous, anxious life, I get angry. And if my genital performance has become somehow symbolic of a whole way of life, at whom might I be angry? Woman surely deserves my anger, for is she not the one inviting me to perform? The longed-for invitation becomes the unconscious threat. Our psychologies complicate our histories.

Another quirk of the male psychological experience regarding women is envy. In spite of centuries of mistaken reproductive biological knowledge, men have always known that in the birthing process women are much more involved with life-giving than they. Birth is awesome, mysterious, powerful, and men have only a remotely connected role. Instead of Freud's theory of women's penis envy (a phenomenon more commonly encountered in the male locker room than in the female psyche), a theory of men's womb envy may be more appropriate. How else can we understand the male symbols of our own birthing powers—the Father God gives birth to the Son, Adam gives birth to Eve, male clergy give birth to new life through baptism—symbols that many men still jealously guard? Envy breeds resentment. Envy of the womb breeds resentment of the one who has the womb. That the resentment is unconscious makes it no less real, only more devious. Our psychologies do complicate our histories.

Sexism is stubborn. It is more complex in origin and continuing dynamics than this brief description suggests. Certain other facets, equally important, will demand our attention later. For now we must just grasp something of that pervasive phenomenon through which not only women but men as well have been damaged.

The damage by and to men has come from fear: deep fears, histori-cally transmitted fears, unconscious fears. Christian spirituality at its best speaks to those fears in ways we might yet claim. To the fear of performance failure, there is a word of grace: our worth need not be, cannot be, earned—it is given. To the fear of the father's world and the remoteness of the transcendent Father, there is a word of God's gender inclusiveness and the pervasive, vulnerable divine im-manence. To the fear of the spontaneous, feeling child within there is the invitation to become like a child—and enter the New Age.

The Genitalization of Male Sexuality

When we who are male think of sexuality, we usually think of "sex," and that means genital experience. We do not think first, or primarily, of sensuousness or of an emotionally intimate relation-ship, though these often enter in at some later point. Rather, our focus is more on sexual acts, acts involving genital expression. In turn, we tend to isolate sex from other areas of life. Sexuality, then, does not mean *in the first instance* loving intimacy, sensuous playful-ness, babies, or the *eros* that draws us into communion with all else. It means a happening, a sexual event involving our genitals. This genitalization also means that our sexual organs are highly important to our male self-images. Though the sexuality books tell us "size isn't important," most men feel otherwise. And impotence is an enormous threat to a man's sense of well-being.

Why does this genitalization seem to be such a part of the male sexual picture? Though biology is not destiny, our sexual bodies as male or as female do encourage certain experiential tendencies. Male genitals are external, visible, and easily accessible to touch. One result is that boys predictably masturbate earlier and more fre-quently than do girls. (One exasperated mother exclaimed, "*Why* did God make my son's arms just long enough to reach down there?") Earlier and more frequent masturbation, in turn, tends to focus and reinforce male sexual feelings in the genitals rather than diffusing those sensations throughout the body. And because masturbation usually is subject to disapproval and even punishment if discovered, boys tend to do it quickly, focusing on the speedy orgasm. This pattern not only establishes the genital focus more solidly but also can lead to later problems of premature ejaculation with the partner.

Particularly in adolescence, a boy often has erections at awkward and unintended times—perhaps just when the teacher has called him to go to the blackboard. Such experiences persuade him that his penis is beyond his voluntary control. It is very much his, but not really part of him. Even Augustine observed that his penis seemed to have a mind of its own, bearing a lust and concupiscence not fully accessible to his willpower. His erection in the public baths at age nine brought lasting embarrassment to Augustine and considerable consequences to later Christian sexual teachings.

Male sexual experience also seems focused in specific acts, acts involving excitement, erection, sometimes penetration, and orgasm. Actions are performed. They are definable experiences that occur at certain moments and places. Our actions always seem more specific than our relationships, which are less localized in time and space and more diffused and broad in their meanings.

The male encounters his penis as an instrument for penetration. If the woman senses her sexuality as more internal and mysterious, a man is inclined to experience his sexual body not so much as that which contains mystery within but more as an instrument for penetrating and exploring a mystery essentially external to himself.

What has all this to do with masculine spirituality? For one thing, it seems to encourage the perception that *mystery is external to the self.* Personally, I know that for most of my life I assumed automatically that the proper object of my spiritual life was really "out there," rather than a mystery dwelling deeply within me. It was something I had to penetrate. My desire was to grasp, to understand, to analyze, and possibly to control and possess. All this seemed true regardless of the particular object of my spiritual quest. So it was with God, the ultimate mystery. God appeared more transcendent than immanent, more beyond than within. If in recent years some of this has begun to change for me, these perceptions are still often dominant. And the emphasis on mystery that is external and radically transcendent of the self has been characteristic of male-oriented theology. Most of us were reared on it.

As I listen to women and read feminist accounts of bodily experience, I am impressed by the degree to which many women seem to experience their sexuality as internal, deep, and mysterious. Penelope Washbourn, for example, says:

> I used to think of creation and the image of God as Creator as one who made, fashioned or shaped. I feel now, however, that the image of creation is best understood as being open to, sharing, participating, working with, surrendering to the movement of life . . . and I feel that through my body, specifically through the natural functioning of my female sexual structures, I have been given a perception of these graceful dimensions.[3]

We men, on the other hand, prone to genitalize, have been more inclined toward an instrumental understanding of our sexuality. Instruments can be very good. Indeed, most men are fascinated by instruments and gadgets of all sorts. But, finally, their value is extrinsic rather than intrinsic. Their value resides in what they are good for in relation to an object or problem external to the instrument itself. The instrument and the mystery finally seem very different from each other. The instrument, however prized, is a means to an external end.

Regarding externality and internality, transcendence and immanence, the Protestant Reformation provides an important and revealing example.[4] In the later Middle Ages, the spirituality of the church was shaped by women as well as by men. A large body of religious literature was being produced by women—nuns, anchoresses, and members of female lay orders. That literature depicted God as inclusive of gender traits. Nurturing, nursing, and feeding images for divine action were common. Following the earlier lead of Anselm, these writings also frequently spoke of Jesus Christ as "our mother," whose agony on the cross was that of a woman in labor giving birth to the whole world. So, also, the medieval image of humanity was surprisingly inclusive. Men easily spoke of their own experience in "feminine" modes, and women were comfortable in the "masculine."

The major reformers, however, strongly shifted religious language to the masculine. Images of God and the divine relationship to creation shifted from the marked immanence of late medieval piety to a marked transcendence. The Protestant emphasis upon justification by faith carried with it a strong emphasis on the Father God whose mighty historical acts in redemption justified the believer quite independently of any human cooperation. The emphasis on predestination and the preference for Word over sacrament as means of God's presence accented a wholly other God who made inscrutable judgments apart from human initiative. Theological language regained a highly masculine flavor, and imagery of the divine, with its transcendence, otherness, and arbitrary judgments, was modeled on the father in the patriarchal family.

The Reformation was also iconoclastic—committed to the destruction of physical representations of the divine, which were deemed idolatrous graven images. Reformation leaders counseled the smashing of the icons—relics, crucifixes, stained glass, and images of the Virgin. For Ulrich Zwingli even church music was idolatrous, and he ordered every church organ in Zurich destroyed. What was voiced in all of this was the charge of idolatry. What was left unspoken (and perhaps was not consciously understood) was that all these physical things were too "feminine." They were material, bodily, emotional, and brought the divine presence into immanent fleshly feeling. That jarred the masculine Reformation mood, a bias toward analysis, criticism, distinction, and rationality.

As well as encouraging externalization of mystery, male genitalization seems to encourage men to prize the qualities of hardness, upness, and linearity. These things are not just part of the male sexual experience but a treasured and celebrated part of it. Erection is pleasure and potency, necessary for sexual "success," and the erection mentality is projected upon the world and what seems to be valuable in it. Consider hardness. In the male world of achievement, hard facts mean more than soft data. Men listen more readily to data from the "hard sciences" than to the soft, seemingly mushy information and theories of the "people sciences." Universities reward their physicians and physicists more amply than their humanities scholars. Consider upness. Computers are "up" when they are functioning, "down" when they are in trouble. When a man's psyche is "up," he is ready for the day's challenges.

Men also honor straightness and linearity. To be sexually straight for a male in a homophobic society is crucial to being a real man. History has always been more important to male-dominated societies than has nature, and history seems to be linear. It appears to move in a line, from here to there, going somewhere different from where it is now. Nature, on the other hand, appears to be cyclical. Seasons and rhythms of life repeat themselves over and over, a phenomenon that men have less understood and valued.

It is no accident that male spirituality, whether formally religious or not, has been more inclined toward ladders than toward circles. Indeed, the ladder image has been one of the most dominant metaphors in western spirituality.[5] Christian mystics took the "up" motif from Hellenistic Greek philosophy, particularly that of Plato and the Neoplatonists, not from the Bible. Here the spirit-body dualism reigned supreme. Through the proper disciplines, the believer moved up the ladder of virtue from the fleshly to the spiritual, from the earthly to the heavenly.

The upness of the ladder image has made its mark on popular pieties through the ages as well as on the more formal spiritual disciplines. Many of us in our youth learned the old Christian camp song, "We Are Climbing Jacob's Ladder." The metaphor is clearly male. Upness dominates ("Every rung goes higher, higher"). The climber has a military image ("soldiers of the cross"). Upness, linearity, externality, and individualism are all mated. One climbs up the straight ladder to reach the prize, which is external. One climbs strenuously and alone (there is room only for one on the ladder). One reaches away from the earthly toward the heavenly. The women's movement in recent years has written a different version, "We Are Dancing Sarah's Circle." The imagery is communal ("Every ring gets fuller, fuller"). Instead of upness, there is groundedness in the earth. Instead of the strenuous climb, it is a celebrative dance. Rather than the defensive or combative military image, the image is one of bonding ("sisters, brothers all"). The contrasts are evident.

The male genitalization of sexual feelings does not automatically cause or rigidly determine a certain shape of masculine spirituality. It seems, however, to *incline* most men toward certain perceptions and emphases: externality, transcendence, hardness, linearity, upness. These shapes and qualities, perceived in Christian terms, have truth to them. But the truth is only partial. Taken as sufficient or normative, these truths become destructive. They can make us sick.

But one of the strange workings of God's grace is our sense of restlessness and dis-ease. Men sometimes feel this about their sex lives. There is something wrong, or something missing. "This is good, but there must be something more than this." It is no accident that the parallel often happens in a man's spiritual experience. For, try as we might, the two parts of our lives simply will not be divorced.

Separation

In sex men seek many different things on many different occasions: pleasure, release of physical tension, excitement, escape from boredom and stress, sensual and physical ecstasy. Beneath and beyond all these, however, is the search for intimacy. But as much as they desire it and occasionally find it, intimacy does not come easily, nor does it seem to be the natural state of things. What does seem natural to men is that individuals are ultimately separate from each other. The gap must be bridged if intimacy is to occur. I believe this is the chief reason behind male concerns about technical performance in sex: Did I do well? satisfy my partner? take my proper responsibility for the success of our lovemaking? It is a window on another major issue in male sexuality: separation.

The debate in recent years about moral development provides an illustration. Harvard psychologist Lawrence Kohlberg, after years of research that included cross-cultural studies, developed a scheme of moral development. It was a model of six stages, moving from the lower to the higher (again a ladder image). The highest stages were characterized by the individual's increasing capacity for rational and reflective understanding of human rights. Kohlberg's colleague Carol Gilligan criticized the scheme. Based as it was on studies of all-male samples, his model was much more a study of male than of human moral development. Her own research indicated that women were much less inclined to view themselves as separated individuals reflecting about individual rights. Far more readily they saw themselves as involved in webs of relationships, the meanings of which were the stuff of morality. She linked the gender difference to basic issues in sexual development.[6]

Nancy Chodorow's pioneering work provides a framework of interpretation for Gilligan and others. Chodorow concludes that

> growing girls come to define and experience themselves as continuous with others; their experience of self contains more flexible or permeable ego boundaries. Boys come to define themselves as more separate and distinct, with a greater sense of rigid ego boundaries and differentiation. The basic feminine sense of self is connected to the world, the basic masculine sense of self is separate.[7]

The fundamental reason for this is that the vast majority of infants and young children receive their primary nurture from a woman, the mother (or a female mother substitute). The father most often stands outside the charmed circle of intense parent-child bonding, a circle on which the infant is profoundly dependent.

There are two basic tasks facing every infant: the establishment of gender identity and the establishment of individuation—who am I as a male or as a female, and who am I as a unique individual? Because of the mother's central role, the processes for resolving these two tasks are significantly different for boys, compared with girls. Girls experience themselves as like their mothers, continuous with them, and the sense of gender identity is a natural flow. On the other hand, "mothers experience their sons as a male opposite," and boys in order to define themselves as masculine must psychically separate themselves from their mothers. As a result, male development involves a "more empathic individuation and a more defensive firming of experienced ego boundaries."[8] Boys define their male gender identities principally through separation and individuation, whereas girls define theirs through attachment and identification. Thus the girl is more apt to be successful in establishing her gender identity but less so in establishing her individuality. It is just the opposite for the boy. For him, gender identity comes less easily and more painfully. But he early develops skills in separation, proficiency in establishing the internal boundaries of the self that set him off from the rest of the world.

The significance of this process for the boy is hard to overestimate. Lillian B. Rubin says it well:

> For a boy who has been raised by a woman, the consolidation of his gender identity requires a profound upheaval in his inner psychic life. In order to identify with his maleness, he must relinquish his identifi-

cation with his mother—the first person to be internalized into his inner psychic world. . . . To protect against the pain wrought by this radical shift in his internal world, the child builds a set of defenses that will serve him, for good or for ill, for the rest of his life . . . boundaries that are fixed and firm.[9]

I believe this has a number of important implications for male sexuality and masculine spirituality. One is the male tendency to separate sex from intimacy. There is some truth to the old adage that men give love in order to get sex while women give sex in order to get love, and some truth to the observation that men more readily can engage in sex without deep emotional attachment. But the explanation is not a higher male sex drive, for which there is no persuasive evidence. Instead, the story seems to lie in the different meanings that males and females have learned to attach to sex and intimacy.

As the boy begins to separate from his mother, his emotional feelings and his erotic feelings gradually separate from each other, and erotic feelings take on a more specifically sexual content. As he seeks his masculinity by separating from his earlier intense identification with his mother, it is the emotional feelings and connections that are pressed down. Sexual feelings (at least for the boy developing more heterosexually) stay largely in place. He does not experience them under attack. It is the emotional connection that is the real threat to his quest for manhood. While his sexual feelings are still directed toward his mother, the incest taboo now makes it clear that any genital expression must take place with women other than his mother. For the girl, at the same time, something opposite is taking place: the emotional feelings toward her mother remain intact, while sexual desire must be repressed and redirected toward men.

The dynamic persists through adulthood. Men tend to respond more quickly to the sexual aspects of a relationship, while women more readily accent the emotional, frequently finding those emotional meanings necessary precursors to their sexual stimulation. Men can tolerate, even enjoy, impersonal sex more readily, for sexual feelings have retained a somewhat independent status for them.

A corollary emerges: Women seem to find emotional attachments that have no genital expression easier to maintain than do men; if a man feels intense emotions, sex seems called for. The contrast between the sexes is understandable because of the particular drive that has been allowed to remain intact between the child and the mother. For the female it was the emotional bond that remained largely undisturbed. For the male it was the sexual, even though that was inhibited from direct expression with the mother by the incest taboo. Whichever bond remained relatively intact in this childhood process apparently can continue to find expression without being joined to the other: sex without emotion or emotion without sex. Thus, if women more readily want emotional attachment prior to sexual involvement with another, they also seem more able to maintain emotionally intense relationships without sexual expression. For men, however, the tendency is different. If sexual feelings can quite readily exist without specific emotional attachments, emotional attachments without sexual feelings are more confusing for the male.

Granted, the realities of concrete individual lives, male or female, are never quite as neat as these theories. Nevertheless, I find such explanations compelling in clarifying what lies behind the different tendencies in men and women. We are still talking about *tendencies,* not determinations. But our inclinations, while they can be modified, are important factors for us.

We can understand, for example, not only why men can more easily separate sex from emotional attachment than can women (and this seems true whether the person is dominantly heterosexual or homosexual). We also have a clue why men find their emotional attachments so frequently depending upon sexual connections. And, to the extent this is true, we can understand why sex becomes the one arena of a man's life where it seems legitimate to express his deeper feelings. We can also see why for heterosexual men deep emotional attachments to other men will seem threatening; such attachments seem to imply sex. The same is not generally true of the heterosexual woman's feelings for other women. And if male sexual feelings tend to have a status quite independent of emotional attachments, we can understand better why boys masturbate earlier and more frequently than girls. I will discuss these issues more fully in chapters to follow. At this point it is simply necessary to recognize the underlying dynamics of the male tendency toward sexual separation. And it is important to recognize that separation is not only a sexual issue but a spiritual one.

These early separation dynamics experienced between boy and mother also play themselves out in the boy's frustrated search for his father. Pushing away and pushed away from his mother in order to find his male identity, he looks for direct and positive clues about manhood from his father (if, indeed, his is a two-parent family). But the father is likely to be more physically and emotionally distant than the mother; gone most of the day, when home he is less emotionally accessible. Thus begins the quest that many men feel throughout a lifetime: trying to find the father.

Since immediate and powerful clues about manhood are less available in the family to the boy than those about womanhood for the girl, he seeks them elsewhere. Cultural images conveyed by the media are one source. Though they are abstract and somewhat unreal, they have some early effect. Yet the boy needs warm flesh-and-blood clues. He seeks them in young male playmates, his peers. But they are as confused as he. So another process emerges: identification of the masculine through negative evaluation of the feminine. What is a boy? Listen on the playground to the answers: "Boys *aren't* girls. They *aren't* sissies. They *don't* cry. They *don't* always run to Mommy." Masculinity is early defined by what it is not. What it *is* is much harder to comprehend.

Intimacy now becomes a threat to the male's struggle for masculine identity. The very thing that he craves, the thing all persons need for nourishing life itself, is a problem. He has established his tenuous hold on masculinity through separation and boundary-making, and emotional closeness threatens that precarious grip.

The possibility of intimacy with women takes on an ambivalent character for the boy and, later, the man. On the one hand he deeply craves it. If he is dominantly heterosexual, his sexual desire is for her, a desire whose fundamental meaning is communion. Furthermore, his fixed and firm ego boundaries have not only circumscribed his relationships and separated his selfhood from others, they have also minimized his connection to his own inner emotional life. Thus, almost instinctively, he knows he needs the woman to be his vicarious emotional expresser and the interpreter of his own feelings to himself. He might have turned to other males for help. But they, like himself, seem less equipped for the task. Further, his homophobic fears demand that he keep emotional distance from them (a subject I will discuss in the next chapter). So he turns for intimacy to the woman. But he approaches her with some wariness and distrust. She represents the very feelings of dependency and vulnerability he has fought so hard to master. Further, she represents the mother whom he had to renounce to find his manhood, the mother who abandoned him to the shadowy world of men when he had depended upon her for life itself.

Typically for the man, then, there is a deep tension between intimacy and masculinity. He wants both, and each seems to be purchased at the price of the other. His search for both is likely to last a lifetime. But in the meantime, if he is to hold onto what manhood he has, he must settle for separation as the basic reality. "It's just the way things are."

Men, Fathers, and God

We have looked at three marks of men's sexual experience: sexism, genitalization, and separation. Surely they are not the whole story, but they are prevalent in and among those of us who are male. These three, and the greatest of these is separation. It is the greatest simply because it undergirds the other two. Sexism, the ideology of patriarchy, posits separation: the higher male separate from and controlling the lower female. Genitalization posits separation: the male genitals separate from the rest of the body and giving a one-sided phallic consciousness to men's reality.

A richer, more fulfilling, more just and peaceful masculine spirituality will depend in no small measure upon new ways of learning to be sexual. Our male biology will not change, and it will continue to give a different cast to both our sexuality and our spirituality from that which women's bodies give to theirs. This is something to be celebrated. Phallic consciousness, however susceptible to its distortions, can be a source of our strength. There is, as Robert Bly has said, "a hairy man," "an Iron John," within the male. There is a deep and dark, instinctual, Zeus-type energy that we men want and need to tap. It seems related to the desire to penetrate and to explore the mystery of otherness, a desire important to human fulfillment.

At the same time, this needs balance through the development of a more receptive and vulnerable male sexuality that will form the grounding for a more receptive and vulnerable masculine spirituality. One important contribution to this will be more active, nurturant fathering. The emotionally and physically distant father who rewards his son with love made conditional on performance expectations contributes to a male shaped for independence but not intimacy, self-protection but not vulnerability, competition but not mutuality. It does not need to be this way. Granted, the institutional and attitudinal changes necessary for men to become more present, nurturing fathers will be slow. It is still a fact that women are virtually always the primary caregivers for infants. "And," writes Lilian Rubin, "no fact of our early life has greater consequences for how girls and boys develop into women and men, therefore how we relate to each other in our adult years."[10]

"Mothering" is a word rich with meaning for us. It conveys the sense of being nurtured in the most elemental and fundamental ways. But what does "fathering" mean? The difficulty we have giving the word meaningful content is symbolic of the problem. Yet these days men from all walks of life speak unashamedly of wanting more intimacy with their children than they had with their own fathers.

The psychological separation from women is a necessary part of achieving male gender identity. But the woman's world is vitally important to the young boy. It feels like the soft, moist, timeless world of the body, the world of holding and caring, the world of the preconscious and the imagination. The man's world feels like distance, performance demands, and machines. What happens? Samuel

Osherson tells us clearly: "We renounce our neediness for women, for the caring, tactile contact, and for pleasure they represent to us, but we can never escape the need, so we try to hold onto them and get our needs met in disguised ways. Yet when we are emotionally vulnerable we feel the rage and fear of having our neediness exposed. That is the consequence of a childhood pattern in which mother is the emotional caretaker and father a distant, instrumental figure."[11]

Families in which the traditional mother-father roles are actually reversed are rare in our society. Of nearly 25 million families in the United States, only 77,000 fathers, less than one tenth of one percent, today are taking the primary parenting role.[12] Career women who leave the "mothering" job to their husbands are often judged harshly, and husbands who assume that role are often treated as embarrassing anomalies. Yet a study of what happened when such role reversal took place reveals some significant things. The children of both sexes developed healthfully. Boys acquired security about their male gender roles and also flexibility about those roles. And the men were profoundly changed by the experience. Many of their values and perceptions of the world changed, and they developed emotional and relational sides of themselves that had hitherto been almost invisible.[13]

Men who have not had the experience of a deeply nurturing father—perhaps most of us—carry something of "the wounded father" within us, right at the core of our own sense of masculinity. It is the internal image of the father as distant, wounded, or angry. We need the healing of that wounded father.[14]

Part of that healing might come from consciously entering into our fathers' histories, finding out what life was really like for them and empathizing with their pain. Then we might begin to realize that they, too, were deprived of intimacy by their fathers, sometimes even more than we. Part of the healing comes from conscious acts of forgiveness and reconciliation. This is more complex if our fathers are dead or if they are physically or emotionally inaccessible, but sometimes it is still possible. And it is possible for healing to come within ourselves even when reconciliation with the father is impossible. That is because what needs to be healed is our internal image of our fathers and the relationship of that image to our own sense of being men. We can understand the poignant reasons why things were the way they were between our fathers and ourselves. With that understanding may come freedom from the sense that we have been betrayed by them, or that we ourselves betrayed them. Then there will be more freedom for us to explore new ways of being male that are genuinely satisfying to *us.*[15]

A critically important part of our process is finding new ways of

God's being God in our experience. Men have been inclined by their male experience to believe that separation rather than connection is the basic reality, the way things are. Connection and relatedness might be "built," like a bridge arduously constructed to span a wide river, but it does not come easily. And it always has to be deliberately imposed on the natural reality of separateness.

God created us in the divine image, and we returned the favor, creating "God" in our own. Traditional male-constructed theism has perceived God as autonomous and unrelated. Transcendent. Wholly other. Sovereign in "His" absolute power. But there is an irony to this theological creation. Male theologians uncritical of patriarchal sexism, who themselves enjoyed and defended ecclesiastical male power monopolies, erected theologies that located all legitimate power in God and virtually none in humanity. God was imaged as male, and that meant power, control, and the demand for obedience.[16]

Many men are hungering for a fuller experience of God than this. Perhaps intuitively we sense that such a God is a "wounded father" we carry inside us, an image of God distant, cold, controlling, unavailable. We have had enough of separation.

Yet healing that wounded God image is complex. The image has served what we thought was our self-interest. When God became male, males were divinized, and patriarchy had cosmic blessing. At the same time, we have resisted that one-sided masculinized deity, for a male God suggests to men their feminization. Language referring to the church has long been feminized: "She is his new creation by water and the word." All of us, men as well as women, are "she"s when it comes to being the church. That feels uncomfortable. Furthermore, a male God penetrates us. But to be penetrated by anyone or anything, even God, amounts to being womanized. It seems tantamount to a man's degradation, literally loss of grade or status.

Men in the church also become confused by the pressures toward sexually inclusive language. To give up God as "Father" is not only to give up male privilege. It also seems to mean giving up on the search for our own fathers, and that is difficult to do, for we know how deeply we long to reconnect with them. On the other hand, we have had enough of certain kinds of fatherhood, and we want a different understanding of God. To embrace the "feminine" in God is to embrace the promise of that deep nurturing presence and immanence that we so need. But it also raises our unconscious anger at the mother who abandoned us and pushed us out into a man's world where the clues and expectations about our own deepest meanings were hard to find. It is all very confusing in the heart of a man's heart.

And I suspect that the reason for the smaller number of men than women in churches lies precisely in these confusions.

Yet God is neither male nor female. God is infinitely more than our sexual experience and awareness. At the same time, the divine reality embraces those genuine strengths that both sexes know—and that each sex knows in its own human fullness. Masculine spirituality now deeply needs to recognize, name, express, and experience the dimensions of God that have lain so underdeveloped in male theology.

We have had enough of separation. We have had enough of the models of divine transcendence that present the Wholly Other in such distant, power-monopolistic, and controlling ways. We yearn for the experience of a paradoxical transcendence that is radical life-giving and nurturing immanence. In a strange way, even the patriarchal religionists of Christian fundamentalism unwittingly recognize this in their pieties of "sweet Jesus."

Paul Tillich once observed that there are two ways of approaching God, "the way of overcoming estrangement and the way of meeting a stranger."[17] In the latter way, we meet a stranger when we meet God. Essentially we do not belong to each other, and the meeting is accidental. We might become friends on a tentative and somewhat contractual basis, but there is no certainty about it. The stranger might disappear. In the other way, however, we discover *ourselves* when we discover God. We discover that which is identical with our deepest and most real selves, even though it transcends us infinitely. It is something from which we have been estranged, but something from which we have never been and can never be finally separated. This way of meeting God, I believe, is gospel—literally, good news.

This is the experience of God I want and need, and I suspect that among men I am not alone. Sometimes feminist women have expressed the vision more adequately than we men have. Then let them help us. Here is Beverly Harrison describing God as "One present who sustains us, gently but firmly grounding the fragile possibilities of our action, One whose power of co-relation enhances and enriches our acts aimed at human fulfillment, mutuality, and justice. In the web of life in which this lovely Holy One is enmeshed with us, personal fulfillment and mutuality are not inherent contradictions."[18] It is a relief to hear that last sentence, for we men so often thought that they were. That is good news.

THREE
Embracing Friendship

Women gather
    Free to chat of impotent husbands
        and not quite forgotten lovers,
    Sharing dreams with old or new friends
        and confiding desperation,
    Baring souls and unburdening hearts,
Then leave relaxed and laughing,
    Promising to lunch again soon,
    Freed from the pain of no one knowing.

Men gather
    Free to boast of the money they've made
        or will make soon—or the women,
    Displaying how strong and controlled they are
        and unafraid of competition,
    Sharing triumphs and hiding themselves,
Then leave with a handshake and "See you around,"
    Bleeding silently within themselves,
    Bearing the pain of no one knowing.[1]

Has the poet, James Kavanaugh, exaggerated the point? Listen to *Washington Post* columnist Richard Cohen. "My friends have no friends," he writes. "They are men. They think they have friends, and if you ask them whether they have friends they will say yes, but they don't really. They think, for instance, that I'm their friend, but I'm not. It's OK. They're not my friends, either. The reason for that is that we are all men—and men, I have come to believe, cannot or will not have real friends."[2]

I have been struck by the lack of literature on friendship in the Christian tradition. Without any trouble, one can find numerous treatises on other virtues and relationships. But apart from the writings of a few medieval monastics, the theme of friendship is largely conspicuous by its absence. The apparent reason? Males have dominated the theological tradition, and men have had problems with friendship—particularly friendship with other men.

Has it always been that way in western culture? Hoping to find brighter chapters, even if outside the Christian tradition, some might point to the ancient Greeks. Didn't they believe that the very life of the *polis,* the city, rested on male friendship? Didn't the men gather at the agora for endless discussion with each other? True, but recall that the classic Greek culture included only adult free males as citizens, hence only they were potentially friends for each other. Furthermore, the Greek ideal of excellence prompted these men to compete and conspire relentlessly against one another for power and status.

If we jump to the Middle Ages and look at the guilds as groups of male friendship and mutual support, we still find exclusivity and hierarchy. If we look in early modern literature, perhaps Nietzsche and D. H. Lawrence get closest to the ideal of male friendship. But Nietzsche saw men capable of friendship only when they were at the same time competing and striving against each other, and Lawrence's picture of the most intense intimacy between men was when they were vigorously wrestling.[3]

What about current evidence? Consider the conclusions of several studies on men's lives. Daniel Levinson claims that adult friendship with either men or women is something rarely experienced by American men.[4] Herb Goldberg writes, "Many men I interviewed admitted to not having one intimate male friend whom they totally trusted and confided in."[5] Earl Shorris notes that in all the literature of business and management nowhere is there a single chapter on friendship. In the hierarchies of corporate life, relationships are always means to the ends of the organization, and relationships get in the way if valued simply for themselves.[6]

The McGill Report on Male Intimacy concludes that the male fear of self-disclosure is pervasive in our society, and that men's relationships are characterized by at least these things:

> That men's friendships with other men tend to revolve around particular tasks, so they have qualifying labels: "a work friend," "a golf friend," and so forth.
> That men are more self-disclosing to women than to other men, and that they tend to rely upon women to be interpreters of their relationships and interior lives.
> That for men sex seems the supreme intimacy, and the notion

of loving someone as an adult peer seems to imply a sexual relationship.

That because they relate competitively to them, fathers have a difficult time disclosing themselves emotionally and vulnerably to their sons.

That men use humor as a guise for intimacy and often as a defense against it.

And that our culture gives men little guidance and few models concerning adult intimacy without genital sexual involvement.[7]

Indeed, we who are men do seem to handle our lives with an activity-and-achievement style, we handle others with a style of dominance and submission, and we handle our psyches with a style that prizes logical and cool levelheadedness. None of these characteristics is particularly conducive to nurturing the capacities for intimacy and friendship.

So goes the litany among the behavioral scientists who have studied men and friendship. How did we get this way? There is also a litany of fairly predictable and plausible answers in the current literature:

We hear about the absent father. When as a small child I had to push away from my mother to establish my masculinity, I became proficient in separation and in establishing my boundaries, but less adept in developing capacities for relatedness and intimacy. And since my father was more absent than present, physically and emotionally, I lacked the model and experience of adult male friendship.

We hear about male socialization. This is simply the way we males have been socialized: to compete and to armor ourselves against the vulnerability and tender emotions upon which friendship depends.

We hear about the contemporary occupational scene (corporate, technological, mobile), which discourages those relationships that are not instrumentally valuable for the organization.

We hear about the havoc male sexism inflicts upon friendship with women. Even though I may depend emotionally upon women, if in some deep ways I distrust and envy them or if I am not really convinced women are men's equals, meaningful friendship is difficult.

We hear about homophobia, the irrational and inordinate fear of same-sex attraction. And we learn that homophobia is a particular problem for dominantly heterosexual males in a still-patriarchal society.

In short, it seems like a dismal story for men. It is no wonder that the pious man, having excluded most other living human beings from consideration as intimate friends, will sing "What a Friend We Have in Jesus" and the humanist male will simply say, "A man's best friend is his dog."

Underneath all explanations for men's difficulty in friendship I believe there lies one pervasive and haunting theme: *fear.* Fear of vulnerability. Fear of our emotions. Fear of being uncovered, found out. So my fear leads to my desire to control—to be in control of situations, to be in control of my feelings, to be in control of my relationships. Then I will be safe. No one will really know my weakness and my vulnerability. No one will really know my doubts. No one will really know that I am not the producer and achiever I seem to be. Therein lies my real terror.

Without self-disclosure there is little self-understanding. I need to interpret myself to you in order really to understand who I myself am. How does a young boy learn to interpret himself and understand his feelings? Developmentally, the mother is closest to the child. Yet as a young boy I am sure I did not disclose my most powerful feelings to my mother because of my need to deal with aggression, anger, and sexuality, all feelings important to my development, and all of them (at least so I thought) threatening to her. So I hid them. Did I disclose them to my father? Usually not. Not only was he less present to me, but also I perceived his love as more conditional. He was the primary adult who held me to performance standards, and there was punishment of some sort when standards were not achieved. So, as a typical male child I let myself be known mainly by participating in activities, testing my skills, my speed, my endurance, and my abilities with the neighborhood group. But what I let be known was my strength. When I cried, I cried in private and even then stifled my unmanly tears.

The pattern persists into adulthood. Psychotherapists typically report that men disclose themselves to other men most easily on the basis of their mutually recognized adequacy and power. Only after establishing himself as "a strong normal male" is a client usually able to acknowledge himself as a person with a problem. And then, paradoxically, his problem typically revolves around his overwhelming need continually to prove himself as "a strong normal male."

The result of this fear of disclosure is that many men become overdependent upon women, particularly one woman, for virtually all their emotional support. In so doing they place an intolerable strain upon marriages and relationships. As Sam Keen says:

Any single relationship that is expected to fulfill every need of two people will become claustrophobic, cloying, swampy. Besides that, there are types of validation and acceptance that we can receive only from friends of the same sex. . . . There are some stories we can tell only to those who have wrestled in the dark with the same demons. Only men understand the secret fears that go with the territory of masculinity.[8]

It is the ancient but always contemporary issue of justification by grace or justification by works. To the extent that we who are men are conditioned to justify ourselves by performance and achievement, it is going to be difficult for us to hear the word of grace, "You are accepted."

And the demons of self-justification are legion. I hold you at arm's distance. I become a reluctant revealer, an emotional evader because you might discover that at my core I am not really self-sufficient and strong. I am a terrifying mix of neediness and strength, of confusion and certainty, but that is hard to admit.

I talk when I should be listening to you, and when I should be talking about what is going on inside me I am quiet, with nothing to say.

I am addicted to performance and winning, not simply because I have been conditioned this way, but also because my conditioning serves my present needs for defense. When I get the big contract or write the book or win the game I am in control, in charge of my life, and have influence over others.

Part of the difficulty, once again, lies in the persistence of masculinism in theological language and imagery, hence in our religious experience. With years of the Fatherhood of God bred into our bones, even the most conscious male has difficulty fully internalizing the divine inclusiveness. And what, for most men, is a father's love? Sons typically know that it is often demanding, unforgiving, and conditional. It is an emotion akin to respect, and like respect a father's love must be earned. When that love is not adequately earned by the son, it is withdrawn. How? The ultimate withdrawal of love is absence, emotional distance underscored by physical distance. And by withdrawing his love, the father conveys two strikingly important lessons of manhood. One is independence: be your own man, keep to yourself. The other is self-protection: keep your guard up.[9]

A distinguished author of both fiction and science acknowledged in a revealing article that through his relationship with his parents, particularly his father, he had become an overachiever, a workaholic and an obsessive self-improver. His father never got around to treat-

ing him as a grown man. Though he lived long enough to see the
son's first two novels, a textbook, and some forty stories and published articles, full approval was never forthcoming. This author is
now over seventy years old and has more than a hundred books to
his credit. Nevertheless, he writes, "So my youthful yearning for
parental approval has never been slaked. Family ghosts still haunt
my cortex."[10] When those family ghosts are projected onto God, the
compulsion toward self-justification can become almost irresistible.

What Do We Need for Friendship?

There are numerous resources in Christian faith for enriching our
capacities for friendship. Unfortunately, many of these have been
underestimated, even denied, by certain interpretations of the faith.
Just why our male-dominated tradition has so often undercut the
very things that men need is a fascinating question in itself. My focus
here, however, is less upon why this neglect and more upon what we
men need.

Self-love

Friendship at its deepest level is always risky and scary. I have to
have a fairly firm grip on myself if I am to let go of myself. If I do
not know who I really am, if I change like a chameleon in response
to changes around me, I will be afraid to open myself to the intense
influences of intimacy because they might dominate and absorb me
completely. If my search for myself still engrosses me, I cannot offer
myself to another person as a gift with no strings attached.

Self-love and self-preoccupation are not the same. In fact, they are
opposites. Christian theology and piety have often been confused at
this point. Self-love has been given a bad press. It has been confused
with selfishness, narcissism, and egocentricity. In fact, authentic
self-love is quite the opposite. The need to grasp, to possess, and to
draw the center of attention to the self is the need of the insecure,
those unsure of their own self-worth. It is the need of those who
perceive love as a closed energy system, existing in only a limited
amount, which then must be hoarded.

Without some measure of genuine self-acceptance, I am tempted
to live with idealized images of myself, shining illusions of perfection.
But such images are protections against my feelings of fragility. And
because the image is unattainable, a vicious cycle emerges: my pride
is hurt, and self-hatred emerges together with the resentment of
others, and then come further attempts to achieve my impossible
ideal and earn their approval—and God's.

The works-righteousness syndrome becomes performance anxiety. Every male knows what that is. It is sexual, to be sure. In order to relate sexually with "success," I must perform. I must be potent, I must achieve an erection, I must be virile. But performance anxiety goes far beyond genital matters. For many men it becomes a whole way of life. And it involves a high degree of self-consciousness, self-judgment, and fear of derision from others. "In performing I split myself into two people, the one doing the performing and the one watching the performance and also watching audience response."[11] But this kind of self-splitting, watching, and judging only produces more anxiety in me and undermines my integrated communion with the other. It is true in the sexual experience. It is also true in every emotionally close human relationship.

While self-love has frequently been assumed to be the irreconcilable opposite of *agape,* or admitted to the Christian life as regrettably inevitable, or justified only if it serves the neighbor, I would argue differently. Self-love is utterly basic to the capacity for friendship. Indeed, self-love and love of the other are of one piece, indivisible. Neither is a means to the other. Quantifying love is misleading. It is not true that the more I save for myself the less I will have for another. Authentic self-love is not a grasping selfishness, nor is it a quest for control. Rather, it is a deep self-acceptance of my own graciously given worth and creaturely fineness, in spite of all of my flaws.

Any kind of true intimacy depends on the solid sense of identity of each of the partners. Otherwise a relationship becomes symbiotic, with one person becoming an extension of the other. Emotional intimacy is always threatening to the person who lacks self-affirmation. Without it, I understand myself only in a social role. Without it, I see myself only mirrored in another's expectations of me, and I turn constantly inward toward my own needs and requirements. With self-love, however, there comes that sense of personal identity which undergirds my possibility of turning outward toward others and exposing the depths of who I am. When such self-love occurs, there is grace.

The realization of such grace is made more possible by our own conscious decisions. One is the decision to try to see myself through the eyes of the Divine Lover, for then I see myself as worthful and beloved. To view myself otherwise is an affront to my Creator. Another is a commitment to the truth that it is just as morally wrong to devalue, dislike, and despise myself as to have such attitudes toward others. Still another important step is learning to accept forgiveness from others, a paradoxical reality that augments my own capacity for self-love.[12]

These things may be hard for many men, conditioned as we are toward self-sufficiency and earned merit. But the intimacy we need and crave depends in no small measure on these movements of grace.

Erotic Love

The ancient Greeks, whose language was more nuanced than ours, had not one word for love but four: *agape* (self-giving), *philia* (friendship), *eros* (the quest for fulfillment), and *epithymia* (sexual desire or libido). In those few places where Christian literature attends to friendship, philia is affirmed but with guarded qualifications. The problem seems to be that friendship is a "preferential love." We are selective in choosing our friends. We prefer some over others. How can this be reconciled with agape, the other-regarding, self-disregarding ideal of Christian love?

The answers have been largely twofold. One is that philia is justified in spite of its being selective because it prepares us for a wider and more embracing love. Good experiences of personal friendship open us up to a larger embrace. The other answer insists that philia depends for its very existence on agape, for without unselfish, self-sacrificing love, friendships would deteriorate into selfishness. Without agape I would simply use the other to fill my own needs. Whatever the argument, the overall message is clear: eros corrupts philia.

The mood of this discussion feels analytical and detached. Missing is the sense of flesh-and-blood experience. In actuality, our friendships, when they are deep and sustained, personal and significant, have a great deal of eroticism to them. Eros is desire. It is the quest for fulfillment through communion with the object of our love. That which we need, which we seek, might be another person. It also might be art, music, nature, God, or countless other sources of attraction. We experience eros when we are drawn to another, when we strongly sense the other's attraction, when we find ourselves both filled and filling in communion with the other. Eros is sensuous and bodily. It has strong emotions. We want to touch, to feel, to experience the other.

Yet many of us who are male have difficulty with the erotic. We have been taught to fear it. It seems associated with passion, with loss of control. We have been told that eros threatens our institutions and social fabric. So we settle for the abstract over the concrete, the cool over the warm, the competitive and combative over the intimate. We keep our feelings, our sensing, our touching under control, even while secretly we yearn. Then the erotic becomes confined to the bedroom, where it seems to belong. Let loose in the rest of our lives it would be unmanly. Thus is eros divorced from philia. But when we banish the erotic from so much of our lives, we also seriously limit our capacities for friendship.

Early in their lives we teach our children to limit the erotic. Yet the developmental pattern of the two sexes is different in this respect.[13] Because a girl and her mother are both of the same sex, the basic emotional quality of the daughter's attachment and identification with the mother remains undisturbed. For the boy it is different. He needs to repress his identification with his mother if he is to establish his masculinity. But this means he also needs to distance himself from attachment to her. Attachment is erotic. It is the desire to bind closely with another. But the boy learns early that the erotic attachment to the most significant figure in his life must be broken if he is ever to become a man. The lesson stays with him into adulthood: eros is dangerous for a male.

The suspicion is reinforced by the either/or thought patterns to which we men are prone. We like to divide things. When thinking of love we fall into this pattern. If there are different aspects to love, there must be discrete and different kinds. Then there also must be better and worse kinds, even good and bad.

We pit agape against eros because of our male penchant for hierarchies, seeing agape higher and other loves lower. Then it is the task of the higher to control (if not eliminate) the lower. Further, agape comes from one who is self-sufficient and strong, hence one who can be self-giving to others. Our logic takes an unannounced twist: not only is it more blessed to give than to receive, it is also easier. A man can stay in control of things when he is not indebted to another, when he is self-sufficient and not needy, when others depend on his largesse, not he on theirs.

But love is multidimensional. Each dimension needs the others for love's wholeness. Without eros, agape is cold and devoid of energizing passion. Without philia, epithymia becomes a sexual contract. Without epithymia, other ways of loving become bloodless. Without agape, the other dimensions of loving lose their self-giving, transformative power.

Eros invites the experience of the holy. It encourages men to loosen their grip on the need to control, and that is both its attraction and its fearfulness. Eros is longing. At its deepest it is the urgent longing of our whole being for communion and connectedness. Communion is holy. But we fear the holy even while we know we must connect with it to be truly ourselves. Still, eros draws us. Sometimes it appears through epithymia, flesh's longing for flesh, and should that loving result in orgasm, for a delicious moment we are thrown out of control. It is the experience men both seek and fear. It is true of intimacy in general. Intimacy does not thrive on patterns of control. It does thrive when control needs are relaxed, when deep desire for connection is admitted. That is an invitation to the holy.

Because eros has strong desire at its core, it invites a whole array of feelings. But, as Wilson Yates observes, feelings are often a man's "briar patch world," where he encounters several characteristic dilemmas: the fear of feelings, the devaluing of them, an absence of feelings, and obsession with them.[14] All intense feelings can be fearful, for they challenge our control, seem to put us at their mercy, even at times threaten to destroy us. One tactic, then, is to devalue and dismiss them. Feelings are women's stuff, unimportant in a man's rational world. Our dismissal can lead to a sense of the absence of feelings. When asked what I am feeling, I quite literally do not know, hence respond with what I am thinking. But another dilemma is possible also. In the jargon of our day, I can develop an obsessive concern for "getting in touch with feelings," an obsession that idolizes them as our life's purpose rather than seeing them as crucial means for understanding our lives. It is a briar-patch world indeed, but eros knows that feelings are essential if intimacy is to grow.

Consider one basic erotic feeling, for example: the sense of neediness. When I allow agape to banish eros, I lose awareness of my own neediness. It is not permitted. It is unbecoming to the agapeic life. But then I am living a lie—the lie of my own self-sufficiency, the lie that I have strength to be the giver only, the lie that I never need to receive. The deception buttresses my need to control, for when I am the giver and the other is the only needy one, I am secure in my superiority. Truly, the words men often find hardest to speak are "I want . . . I need . . . I can't . . . I'm afraid."

Dietrich Bonhoeffer struggled with this from his prison cell. Not long before he was hanged by the Nazis, the remarkable theologian wrote a haunting poem, "Who Am I?" In it he spoke of the impressions others seem to have had of him—that he was always strong, cheerful, proud, "like one accustomed to win." But then come these lines:

> Am I then really all that which other men tell of?
> Or am I only what I know of myself,
> restless and longing and sick, like a bird in a cage,
> struggling for breath, as though hands were compressing my throat,
> yearning for colours, for flowers, for the voices of birds,
> thirsting for words of kindness, for neighbourliness,
> trembling with anger at despotisms and petty humiliation,
> tossing in expectation of great events,
> powerlessly trembling for friends at an infinite distance . . . ?

That is shamelessly admitted eros. Though my comfortable situation is far different from Bonhoeffer's, still in the prisons of my own construction I identify with him. His poem ends:

> Who am I? This or the other?
> Am I one person today, and tomorrow another?
> Am I both at once? A hypocrite before others,
> and before myself a contemptibly woebegone weakling?
> Or is something within me still like a beaten army,
> fleeing in disorder from victory already achieved?
>
> Who am I? They mock me, these lonely questions of mine.
> Whoever I am, thou knowest, O God, I am thine.[15]

There is relief in admitting neediness. There is relief in admitting that I am not self-sufficient, that I am not always strong, cheerful, proud, or a winner. There is a strange, paradoxical strength in claiming my eros, my incompleteness, my yearning, my thirsting, my desire, my trembling for friends.

In the midst of all this there is the grace of knowing that finally we are God's. Not agape only, the Cosmic Lover is also emotional, desirous eros. Albert North Whitehead spoke of the "Divine Eros" in the universe as "the living urge toward all possibilities, claiming the goodness of their realization."[16] This Divine Eros frequents our world, incarnating itself in surprising ways, not the least of which is that desire we name friendship.

Play and Pleasure

The recovery of eros is also a recovery of play, an important dimension of friendship. In spite of so much apparent hedonism around us, our society frequently devalues play for adults, especially for adult males. We have imbibed deeply of the Calvinist work ethic as central to our sense of self and worth. Play is a waste of time to the breadwinner. In a world where intellect, power, and work success define "the man," men have become playfully constipated. At best we work hard at playing, improving our golf game, pummeling the body into submission at the Nautilus machine, taking the extra tennis lesson. But the play that is nonviolent, noncompetitive, spontaneous, creative, pleasurable, and without a goal or task orientation is suspect.

The recovery of play is an invitation to friendship. Playfulness means the devaluation of control. Play involves the capacity to trust and to surrender to the moment. So also with friendship. Friendship has no achievement agenda, no task orientation, and this may be something difficult for men to learn. A case in point: Mary calls her friend Jane, proposing that they lunch together. Jane's likely response: "Of course, Mary, I'd like that. When shall we get together?" John calls Bill, proposing lunch. Bill's likely response: "Sure, John, what's up? What's on your mind?" Here togetherness needs to be justified by a task or an agenda. It seems suspect if it is valued just for itself.

Of course friends often do things together. They embark on common tasks and tackle common agendas. They stand side by side facing something to be done. Indeed, some suggest that men have their own distinctive style of relating: it is shoulder-to-shoulder rather than face-to-face. But must it be an either/or proposition? Friendship often means letting loose of the task, letting go of the need to prove one's usefulness. It means valuing the presence of the other just for the other's own sake. It is enough just to be, and to be with. That is playful. And that is gracious.

The recovery of eros and its playfulness means the recovery of pleasure. Friendship both depends and thrives on it. But the Christian tradition has shied away from a positive embrace of pleasure. Long ago, when the two sexual dualisms (spirit over body, and man over woman) joined together, the antipleasure stage was set. "If it feels good, it must be wrong." Pleasure of all sorts seemed bodily, hence suspect. And because pleasure was not something of the spirit or the mind, it was suspect for men. So the chapters of our history on this matter unfolded, and attitudes about sexual pleasure became formative for matters of friendship.

The Roman Stoics, who so influenced early Christianity, prized a life devoid of passion. Some early Christian Stoics, following their lead, wished that sexual intercourse (obviously necessary for the continuation of the race) might be as passionless as urination. Medieval theologians were largely suspicious of sexual pleasure because in orgasm people seemed to lose their rationality, and to the medievalist, rationality was the key to human dignity. The Protestant Reformers of the sixteenth century abandoned the notion that celibacy was a higher virtue than married love, but they could not quite believe that sexual pleasure was a good in its own right. It still remained God's enticement to procreation. The nineteenth-century Victorians simply assumed that sexual pleasure was animalistic.

Each of these antipleasure chapters in the book of church history was dominated by male thought. In fairness to the Christian tradition, it must be said that some of the ascetical practices were predicated upon rather sophisticated understandings of bodily addictions and upon surprisingly contemporary insights into methods of focusing energy and expanding consciousness.[17] Nevertheless, assumptions about the self as a closed energy system were even more pronounced: the idea that the soul gathers energy at the expense of the body, and the belief that the more the body is experienced the less the soul will be. The soul withers without strict bodily discipline.

Yet my experience is often different from this. To experience the heights of sexual pleasure I must let loose of my need to control. I must let go, giving myself over to the delicious moment. It is a paradox, known in other ways in the gospel but applicable here as well: losing the self means finding the self. Sexual pleasure nurtures the reunion of the self with the self. My body, so often alien and disconnected, becomes me again. I not only experience myself, I experience love for myself and recover a sense of the goodness of being alive.

These phenomena of pleasure seem true not only of the sexual experience at its best but also of friendship. My friend and I may be paddling a canoe on a quiet lake or exploring a strange city together or sitting down to a good meal. In the midst of giving myself over to the experience, there seems to be a spontaneous movement from my own enjoyment to my enjoyment of my friend. It is not that my consciously altruistic attitudes direct me to give my friend pleasure. Rather, my own pleasure and that of my friend coincide and mutually enhance each other. A remarkable spiral of pleasure ushers in a gracious experience of communion.[18]

The paradoxes of pleasure and friendship echo in a variety of ways the paradoxes of Christian faith itself. Listen to one psychiatrist:

> Pleasure cannot be possessed. One must give one's self over to the pleasure, that is, allow the pleasure to take possession of one's being. Whereas the response of pain involves a heightening of self-consciousness, the response of pleasure entails and demands a decrease of self-consciousness. Pleasure eludes the self-conscious individual, as it is denied to the egotist. To have pleasure one has to "let go."[19]

In this quotation we could substitute the word "friendship" for "pleasure" and the word "loneliness" for "pain," and the statement would be just as true and compelling. That suggests something of great importance to men—we who are conditioned to stay in control. But by the grace of God it is possible. And it is to be treasured and savored.

Dealing with Homophobia

The recovery of our eros is fundamental to coping with our homophobia too. Homophobia, the extreme and irrational fear of same-sex attraction, is rampant among most dominantly heterosexual men. (I use the qualifying word "dominantly," for it is likely that few if any persons are completely heterosexual or completely homosexual.) Homophobia is clearly a major barrier to emotional intimacy in male-male friendships, including that of fathers and sons.

It is both stubborn and complex. Dr. George Weinberg originally coined the term in 1972. He identified homophobia as a personal and social dynamic involving dread of same-sex attraction and erotic expression, as fear of being physically close to a same-sex–oriented person, as self-loathing by someone who is gay or lesbian, and as generalized irrational fear of homosexuality.[20]

Others think that the term "heterosexism" is more useful.[21] Sometimes we too easily identify a phobia with other people only, believing it to be a morbid, hysterical, private abnormality we ourselves do not have. Since the term "heterosexism" points to the political and institutionalized dynamics that enforce the notion of compulsory and normative heterosexuality, it is useful in reminding us of a pervasive dynamic that affects us all. This is an important reminder. I will use the term "homophobia"—but with this point in mind: the dynamic is not only deeply personal but also deeply institutionalized as a political and social ideology.

It is not my intent to deal with biblical issues around homosexuality here.[22] Yet two things are worth noting briefly. One is that on no other moral issue today is there such selective literalism in biblical interpretation as that of homosexual expression. Second, we hear it said that many Christians honestly and sincerely find homosexual expression contrary to God's will on biblical grounds which are not literalistic but which are carefully and consistently used. To these folk, some will say, the term "homophobia" is unfairly applied. But this seems similar to believing that it is not possible to label a white person as racist who carefully and honestly grounds in biblical interpretation the belief that blacks are subhuman.[23] Honesty, sincerity, and elaborate uses of scripture are no defense against homophobia. We are—all of us—afflicted with the disease.

But males, at least in our culture, seem to be more afflicted than do women. Why? One important reason, noted earlier, is that males generally are more distanced from their bodily experience and feelings in our society than are females. One of the consistent research findings in this area is that the more I am dissociated from a strong and positive sense of my body, the more I will tend to be dichotomous in my thought patterns. In other words, body dualism correlates with perceptual dualism. I will be inclined to populate the world into rigid "either/or's": we/they; good/bad; black/white; communist/capitalist; male/female. It is *either* homosexual or heterosexual. With an either/or perception of reality, there is little tolerance for ambiguity.

But the fact of the matter, according to sexological research, is that very few of us are either exclusively heterosexual or homosexual. Years ago, well before the "sexual revolution," Alfred Kinsey startled the American public with his discovery that at least 50 percent of the male population and 28 percent of females engage in homosexual genital behavior at some time in their lives. And for 37 percent of American males, it is orgasmic behavior in postadolescent, adult years.[24] Furthermore, sexual orientation is not measured simply by genital behavior. It has many other variables as well: sense of attraction, fantasy, self-identification, emotional preference, the preferred sex for one's social interaction, and general life-style. And all of these are subject to change and variation over an individual's life span.[25] While most of us clearly prefer one sex more than the other in our genital experience, in feelings, fantasies, and desires for physical closeness we have more of a mix within us than we usually recognize. Lacking this recognition, however, what happens? As a male predisposed to either/or dichotomies in understanding sexual orientation, as one programmed by religion and society to believe that heterosexuality is normative, I still get some same-sex feelings. But because of my conditioning, I find them intolerable. So I project my rejection outward onto those visible symbols, gay males, punishing them for what I feel in myself but cannot tolerate.

A related dynamic is my envy of gays' sexual power. As one who because of typical male experience feels somewhat distanced from his intimate bodily reality, I am also one whose sexuality is largely genitalized. I am one whose conditioning makes him think that the real man is always ready for sex, that he can never get enough of it, and that his potency is the ultimate symbol of his manliness.

However, deep within and unconsciously, I live with the fear of impotence. Every man does. To be sexually "successful," he has to "get it up and keep it up." And the genitalized symbolism of manly success becomes the symbolic clue to a whole life-style. It is a life made worthful by one's potency—in relationships, in work, in athletics, in politics. But impotence (sexual or otherwise) is always lurking in the wings. And every man somehow knows it. Because of the very nature of sexual stereotyping, however, homosexual people are seen by others through a primarily genital, in-bed focus. Hence, whether they are butchers, bakers, or candlestick makers, whether they are Presbyterians, Catholics, or agnostics, they are seen primarily as genital sexual actors. And precisely because of that stereotype, I am inclined to see them as more sexual, and more potent, than I am. While in my conscious stereotype, I think of the gay male as "less of a man" than I, in the confusions of my homophobic unconscious, I see him as *more* male than I. Homosexuality, particularly gay

homosexuality, has become the primary symbol of sexual energy and
potency, freely expressed. It has become the primary symbol of
potency, of the one who is always ready. Thus, in a strange way, the
gay male is more male than I, and that is the occasion for rage.

But, says my unconscious reasoning, he is *not* really more male
than I! And here enters another dynamic of sexist dualism. If the
male is normative, as he is in patriarchy, the gay male threatens me
because he embodies the symbol of woman. Why? Stereotypically, I
assume that in gay-male sex, one of the partners must be passive, the
receiver, hence "the woman." But the very possibility that a man
would willingly submit to womanization is a symbolic threat to every
other man in a patriarchy.

The gay male threatens me with womanization in still another
way. I know he has the capacity to view me not primarily as a person
but as a sex object, a desired body. But this is how heterosexual men
so frequently have viewed women—as objects. Hence, by his very
existence (quite apart from any overt actions), the gay male disturbs
me by reminding me that I have made sex objects of other human
beings, women, and now I might be treated similarly, hence womanized.

Still another dynamic connects homophobia with my male sexism.
It seems to be a constant of human nature that all people need
validation and affection from their equals. But in a sexist society,
those men who embrace male dominance have only other men as
their equals. To seek validation, love, and affection from other men,
however, is a fearful thing, for we have been taught to relate to other
men on a different basis—competition. The gay male who symbolizes
affection, openness, and the vulnerability of man to man symbolizes
what seems to be denied to the heterosexual male. He then receives
resentment for having that which other men desire and need, but
know they cannot have. So the straight man turns to women for his
emotional validation. Often he leans exclusively upon one woman,
his partner, loading upon her all his emotional baggage. Then he
resents her because she cannot meet all his emotional needs; the load
is too heavy for any one person to carry for another. He resents her,
moreover, because by definition she cannot adequately give what she
has been asked to give: the validation from an *equal.*

I have focused here on male homophobia directed primarily toward gay males for two reasons. First, in a patriarchy it is the
dominant expression of homophobia. When the male norm seems
threatened, those who seem to threaten it must be attacked; "queer
bashing" is directed at gays much more than at lesbians. A second
reason is that male homophobia about males particularly undercuts
the rich possibilities of men's friendship with other men.

Nevertheless, male sexism also erupts in the despising of lesbians. Some of the dynamics are different. Many men can become sexually aroused by the fantasy of women making love with each other, a common portrayal in *Playboy* and *Penthouse*. Those same magazines, for reasons obvious in male homophobia, would never under any circumstances portray male-male sex. But those pictorial fantasies of woman with woman do not really threaten. They can arouse a man's sexual imagination without producing anxiety, because the subjects are already women. They cannot lose the status they do not have, nor can they cause the male viewer to feel his status threatened. After all, these women are playing at sex with each other primarily for men's pleasure. They arouse and entertain the male precisely because their sexuality is trivialized. On the other hand, true (not fantasy) lesbians are indeed threatening to straight males in any patriarchy. They are the living symbols of woman's independence of man. They represent the possibility that women just might not need men for their fundamental validation, sexually or otherwise.

These, then, are some of the dynamics of homophobia in a dualist society. Several things stand out to me. One is the deprivation of men's male friendships. Relationships of a man with other men are so often limited to competition, task cooperation, and "buddyship." The emotional vulnerability required for deep friendship is frightened away. Most men feel that genital sex is the supreme intimacy between people, and if that is true normal men cannot have intimate male friends. Thus, homophobia also impedes the relationships of fathers and sons, with fathers fearing the expression of too much affection and with sons learning to put on their emotional armor. It limits men's development of many of their interests, out of the fear that following certain inclinations will imply homosexuality. One man summarized it trenchantly, reflecting on his experience in men's groups: "The theme, sounded time after time, is this: 'A large segment of my feelings about other men are unknown or distorted because I am afraid they might have something to do with homosexuality. Now I'm lonely for other men and don't know how to find what I want with them.' "[26]

Another thing that claims our attention is the fragility of "manhood" in so many males. One of the consistent findings in the current research is that homophobia is more intensely experienced among those who make sharp and rigid distinctions between masculinity and femininity. Those who do not have a secure feeling about their own gender often insist upon strict gender definitions. Also evident are the many homophobic dynamics that are deeply rooted in male sexism. Homophobia functions as the guardian of a male-defined code of masculinity in a patriarchal society, and the gay male both seems to symbolize "woman" and seems to threaten womanization to any man who acknowledges the acceptability of same-sex feeling.

Further, homophobia simply reminds us of the generalized fear of sexuality in our culture. Nor are men (who are supposed to love sex) exempt. Indeed, the male-dominated theological tradition of Christianity has neglected, ignored, often denigrated the sexual body. And it is homosexual persons (seen through stereotypes) who symbolize positive, exuberant sexuality. In doing so they arouse not only envy but also fear.

Still further, the gay male is resented because he symbolizes the intimacy of men with men, which all men desire but few seem to have. So I punish in others both what I desire and what I also fear in myself. Thus, homophobia strikes most men because we feel in the depth of our own beings our desire for closeness to other men, emotionally and physically even if not genitally. So the resentment against gay males builds. And it builds in all of us regardless of our sexual orientation, for gays inevitably internalize homophobia in a homophobic society, and it becomes self-rejection.

But God's grace embraces both our erotic fears and our erotic longings. That is the good news. I desire closeness with other men. I want their emotional and physical touch. That is who I am, and that is graced. Research suggests that all of us have more bisexual capacities than are usually admitted. It took me many years to recognize and affirm this in myself. The fact that I know myself to be dominantly heterosexual is beside the point. What I now can affirm, and some years ago could not, is that emotionally I want and need closeness with men as well as with women. I have come to believe that the affirmation of the full range of our unique erotic emotions is crucial for expanding our capacities for friendship. And I have come to understand that growth in the ability to affirm the fuller range of my own eros is, indeed, a gift of grace.

Friendship with God

The need for human friendship is natural, given to us in the grace of our creation: "It is not good that [human beings] should be alone" (Gen. 2:18). In the goodness of our sexuality and our created eros we reach out for each other. But in the woundedness and distortions of our sexuality, our capacity for friendship depends on the grace of redemption.

Grace in both our creation and our redemption is always full of paradox, in a host of ways. For men, it is paradoxical that God is sexually inclusive. Though male hegemonies of power have been undergirded by the doctrine of God's maleness, the strange grace is that men deeply need and want something different. Men who have wrestled throughout their lives with the ghosts of their fathers want something different. It is paradoxical that self-love and the capacity to love the other are so intimately intertwined. But that is a gracious realization. It is paradoxical that the recovery of the erotic in our neediness, in our bisexual emotions, in our capacities for play and pleasure, has so much to do with philia, our capacities for friendship.

There is one more paradox needing mention. In order to be capable of friendship, somehow I need to *have* a friend. The friend I need is one who confirms me, confronts me, and celebrates me.[27] When others confirm me, I feel firm on my own ground. I know that as they stand before me they are really *for* me. They will not pull out the rug from under my feet, nor invade the sacredness of my own being. They affirm my own needed space and my own unique style.

Nevertheless, my friend also confronts me, challenging me to acknowledge the ways in which I am being destructive toward myself or others. Confrontation is not just condemnation. My friend does not just condemn me for having a vice, but urges me to resist it. My friend does not simply point to a life-denying tendency within me, but also calls upon me to draw upon the life-affirming resources that are within and around me.

If friendship involves confirmation and confrontation, it also involves celebration. These three, but the greatest of these is celebration. When I look on another as close friend, I celebrate that other's very existence. My friend's unique way of expressing life evokes feelings of thanksgiving in me. My friend's breakthroughs toward fuller and more creative life evoke rejoicing in me. Just as my friend's times of discouragement and despair can draw me out of my own preoccupation and elicit my reaching out in care, so also my friend's "highs" can draw me into celebration. In a good liturgical word, friends not only celebrate each other, they also "concelebrate" life around them.

If these are accurate dynamics of human friendship, they may also be a clue to friendship with God. Alfred North Whitehead once observed that the great religious revolution of the self is when I move from the experience of God as a void, to God as my enemy, finally to God as companion or friend.[28]

Surely, it is the friendship of God to which the Christian affirmation of grace points. If we say that God loves us, what we are saying is that God confirms us, God confronts us, God celebrates us. And when we have experienced that kind of friendship, that kind of acceptance, even if momentarily, we know that everything is transformed and we can never be quite the same again. Even though we slip back into our self-rejecting, self-proving, defensive ways, still we have known what it means, at least for a moment, simply to accept the fact of our acceptance, to have been confirmed, confronted, and celebrated as a friend by the Heart of the universe.

But the final paradox of all is that the Heart of the universe continues to be enfleshed. Under the impact of male theology, for centuries we have been led to believe that the divine incarnation really occurred just once, two thousand years ago. We have confined the Christ to that one human figure: Jesus. As I understand him, however, it was not Jesus' purpose to monopolize the Christic experience but, quite the opposite, to release its reality and power in the world—the meeting with God in and through human flesh.

Thus, in the experience of the depths of friendship with another human being, I literally do experience the friendship of God. It is not an experience somehow "like" God. It is neither an analogy nor a sermon illustration. It *is* God, even if fragmentarily, partially, and with distortion. It still *is* God. This is not an unchanging God of perfection whose divine love is utterly different from human love, whose divine body is utterly different from human bodies.

It is the God experienced in Jesus' parable of the Last Judgment (Matthew 25). "Lord, when did we see thee hungry or thirsty or a stranger or naked or sick or in prison?" Here is the stunning reversal. Now the God-made-flesh seems to be in the wrong place, full of need, full of yearning, full of humanness. But that is the God we meet in our friends and in ourselves. It is that paradoxical God at the center of every friendship—the God yearning, the God savoring, the God playing, the God needing, the God pleasuring, the God confirming, confronting, and celebrating. If this is a different experience of God from that which many men have intimately known, to meet this One in the midst of friendship, and to become capable of friendship because we have met this One, will be gift indeed. To love another human being is perhaps the most difficult and needed of all our human possibilities. To love God in the very midst of loving another human being is sheer gift—and revelation.

FOUR
Embracing Mortality

It is no secret. We live in a violent society. The facts are well known, and we need not rehearse the sobering litany of rape, murder, assault, spouse abuse, child abuse, homophobic violence, racist violence, the power of the gun lobby, military interventions, nuclear arms buildup, and violent ecological abuse. Indeed, every thirty-one seconds someone somewhere in the United States becomes the victim of violent assault. One other fact is also well known but, curiously, not well examined: the overwhelming preponderance of this violence comes from the hands and hearts of *men*. Even cross-cultural studies put the incidence of male violence at four to twenty times higher than that caused by females. And male violence turns inward as well. More male Vietnam veterans have died through self-destructive behavior since returning from that war than died in combat itself.

The issue of violence is an issue of both male sexuality and masculine spirituality. To understand it better, we need to grapple with the ways in which men deal with death. We who are men cope with death in a paradoxical way. On the one hand, we avoid it. It is no surprise, for example, that a male-dominated medical profession is a death-defying, death-denying profession. In spite of all the progress made in understanding the difference between saving life and prolonging the dying process, male physicians still frequently see death as defeat and use all their technological wizardry to stave it off at any cost, regardless of the quality of life.

Personally, I know what it means to be a death avoider. As a typical male I was conditioned early to put on my armor as defense against all attack, physical and emotional, and I learned my lessons well. Big boys don't cry. Be a good soldier. Soon after college when, literally, I was a soldier, my father suddenly died. I was stationed two thousand miles away. I had never seen him sick, and I refused to go to the mortuary to see his body. I wanted to remember him as I had last seen him—hale and hearty, alive, not dead. Nor could I really grieve then, for big boys don't cry, and surely good soldiers don't. (My dad had been a highly decorated veteran of World War I, and the soldier messages in my youth had been strong.) Only years later did I realize how symbolic it was that I chose to attend my father's funeral in uniform. It was almost twenty-five years after his death before I got in touch with my tears, my grief, and my anger, all of which I had been carrying all that time. Such are the death-denial skills of many men. Surely, those skills have been mine.

On the other hand, we men seem to embrace death, particularly violent death, with fascination. The male-controlled media are full of it. Gratuitious violence sells well, and pornographic sexual violence is a huge American industry. In whatever form they appear, death and violence seem to be particularly, even admirably, masculine.

There is a clear history of the fascination of the white male with death and violence in American culture. For the first two hundred years of our country, there was a romanticizing of death.

> The Puritan child . . . was immersed in death at the earliest possible moment: his spiritual well-being required the contemplation of mortality and the terrifying prospects of separation and damnation. The child of the nineteenth century was also taught about death at virtually every turn, but rather than being taught to fear it, he was instructed to *desire it,* to see death as a glorious removal to a better world and as reunion with departed and soon-to-depart loved ones.[1]

While some of today's attitudes about death are different, they still illustrate the point. The air-conditioned tombs of Forest Lawn with piped-in music, slumber rooms, and Beautyrama Adjustable Soft-Foam Bed Caskets, the parents who refuse to discuss death with their children much as their parents refused to discuss sex with them—all these might seem to suggest a swing of the pendulum to the other extreme. But whether we romanticize or deny death, we show our extraordinary discomfort.

What of our attitudes toward violence? While I enjoy watching professional football, I am also concerned about it as a primary and distorted image of American masculinity.[2] Here is a definition of the real man, aggressive and dominant. The virtues of toughness and insensitivity are celebrated, while the woman is clearly on the sidelines, consigned to cheering, squealing, and supporting. It is a controlled violence, played by certain rules, rules defined and celebrated by males. Yet it is a violence that betrays anxieties and contradictions. For all its celebration of bodily toughness, it depends upon dissociation from the body—not listening to its feelings of tiredness or pain or tenderness. It fosters and symbolizes the polarization between men and women: males pummel each other in order to avoid relating to females. It is the Superbowl cult, and as American as apple pie. And it represents much of our economic and political and racial life.

Our political history is replete with clues about masculinity and violence. Theodore Roosevelt became a symbol of the virile male triumphing over physical weakness. He was also the champion of war as the test of manhood. In 1895, alarmed by the closing of the frontier and the rise of the first chapter of the women's movement, he became convinced that what America needed was a good war to make men men again. And America got it. Later, on the eve of World War I, once more Roosevelt saw war as the greatest test of moral and physical manhood. Attacking the hesitancy of Woodrow Wilson to enter the European conflict, he said, "Wilson has done more to emasculate American manhood and weaken its fiber than anyone else I can think of."[3] When the United States declared itself at war in World War II, another Roosevelt's administrative assistant said, "America has become magnificently male again." And a leading war hero, George S. Patton, declared, "All real American men love to fight."

So also the cult of "toughness" has dominated our national administrations in the years since. The Kennedy emphasis on personal toughness is well documented. Presidents Johnson and Nixon could not face being the first American presidents to lose a war, regardless of the consequences. And each of them characterized males who were opposed to tough militarism in terms likening them to women and homosexuals, something to be despised. The Reagan Administration needs little comment.

The Shaping of Male Attitudes

There is no persuasive scientific evidence to date that can explain the preponderance of male violence in terms of biological predisposition. There are some data, though inconclusive at present, suggesting that hormonal differences might make for a modest difference in aggressiveness. But the major factor is clearly social influences. Violence is very largely a learned behavior. For one thing, it is learned by men as a way of proving their masculinity. Most crimes in the United States are committed by males between ages thirteen and twenty-four, a time when such proof seems important.[4]

Violence and death, in some large measure, are sexuality questions. To be sure, sexuality appears to be vastly different. It represents life, vitality, and energy, and violence destroys these precious things. Sexuality symbolizes beginnings; death is an ending. But eros and thanatos are deeply intertwined. In both the experience of sex and death, there is a letting go. In both there is an invitation and a threat in terms of loss of identity and absorption into something else. In both there is raised the radical question of the meaning of our existence. In both there is a pornography, and in both a curtain of silence drawn around frank and open discussion of the subject.

The basic clue to male problems with violence and death lies, I am convinced, in the sexual dualisms that sunder spirit from body and establish a hierarchy of male control over women and all things perceived as feminine. The Christian tradition is full of the evidence.[5] Early theologians of the church, disquieted by their own bodily existence, projected onto women uncontrollable sensuality and responsibility for the fall. Tertullian, addressing women, made it painfully clear: "You are the devil's gateway. You are the unsealer of that forbidden tree. You are the first deserter of the Divine Law. . . . On account of your desert, that is death, even the Son of God had to die."[6] Augustine perceived the male alone as in the image of God, and the woman participating in that divine image only when joined to a husband: "Woman together with her husband is in the image of God. . . . But when she is referred to . . . alone, then she is not the image of God. But as regards the man alone, he is the image of God as fully and completely as when the woman too is joined with him in one."[7]

Roger de Caen, a medieval French monk, provides an extreme example of the body-woman denigration: "If her bowels and flesh were cut open, you would see what filth is covered by her white skin. If a fine crimson cloth covered a pile of foul dung, would anyone be foolish enough to love the dung because of it? There is no plague which monks should dread more than woman: the soul's death."[8]

Centuries later the Protestant Reformers, while expressing more appreciation for women, nevertheless continued to identify them as subordinate in status and particularly identified with the suspect, sensuous body. Luther was particularly so inclined. While in many ways earthy and candid about sexuality and bodily functions, he nevertheless found sexual desire to be a disgraceful result of sin, with women as the primary locus of the problem: "Women are ashamed to admit this, but scripture and life reveal that only one woman in thousands has been endowed with the God-given aptitude to live in chastity and virginity. A woman is not fully the master of herself."[9]

Death, Violence, and the Distancing of the Body

Our bodies are the seat of our emotions. Yet we who are men have been conditioned to distance ourselves from both. We have been taught by our culture to "tough it out" and be in control of ourselves. A counselor in a treatment program for violent men reflects on his clients:

> Boys don't learn to express feelings, which makes it difficult to feel comfortable in intimate relationships. In intimate relationships you must be vulnerable. The men who batter say they want to be close to their wives, but it frightens them because in adulthood it evokes homophobic feelings; it is identified as womanly, which is so frightening. The men articulate this by saying, "That's for women."[10]

The emotional damage done to men through the deprivation of feelings is enormous, and it takes its toll in violence. Joy M. K. Bussert declares, "After listening to the stories of countless women in shelters, and after sitting in on several treatment groups for violent men, *I can only conclude that battering—at least in part—is a substitute for tears.* As little boys, men are taught that 'big boys don't cry,' and that when threatened or hurt they should learn to 'stand up and fight like a man.' Being deprived of human tears, they, in turn, victimize women as a means to live out this impossible cultural assignment to control the feminine within themselves."[11] Thus men who are violent are also victims, raging against a culture that has locked them into an emotional vacuum.

Men's military experience is particularly illustrative. War, observes James Boen, is "the ultimate boys' fairy tale," with its elements of risk, adventure, heroism, rescue of those in distress, and ritualized passage into manhood.[12] The socialization of the soldier is simply an exaggeration of typical masculine socialization in our society. In the military, the attitudes inculcated in males generally in our society are simply magnified and honed to a fine edge. Steeling the recruit against his emotions, hardening his willingness to exercise violence and inflict death, works best on young men still unsure of their own identities. I vividly remember the bayonet assault course in infantry basic training during the Korean War. I can still hear the drill sergeant shrieking, "Kill! Kill! Kill!" while at the same time he used sexual epithets to degrade any soldier whose violence was less than persuasive.

Thus in military socialization there is a systematic effort both to attack and to mold the young man's sexuality. During basic training he is continually threatened by the awesome, intimidating drill instructor, who screams into his face epithets identifying him as homosexual or feminine, while he must remain utterly passive under threat of physical violence. When sexual identity is sufficiently threatened, psychological control is achieved and the young man's sexuality is linked with military functions of aggression and dominance. These are the definition of masculinity; "the army will make a man out of you."

Masculine socialization typically prizes thinking over feeling, and abstraction over concreteness. The result disguises both violence and death, which are very feeling and concrete events. Socialization into cerebral abstraction in turn is closely linked with our body attitudes. Our body attitudes significantly shape the way we will deal with an often confusing world. If I have been conditioned to treat my body as lower and instrumental, as something to be disciplined and controlled, as that which is irrational and must be mastered, that which bears the intimations of decay and mortality, then I will have a certain "feel" for the world. The world "out there" will take on the same kind of half-known, confusing qualities. It will be full of mysterious things that smack of badness. I will resist ambiguity. I will seek simple and clear answers for things and, as we have seen, the world will become populated with dichotomies.

Dichotomizing invites us into a world of abstractions. Daniel Maguire has observed that "only a man could have stood in the ashes of the totally destroyed village of Ben Tre during the war in Vietnam and announce as one colonel did: 'We had to destroy this village in order to save it.' Womanly experience does not fit women to miss the disconnection between ashen destruction and saving."[13]

Abstraction and emotional distancing result in the depersonalization of the enemy. A Vietnam veteran observes that the distancing is both physical and linguistic. Not only do the weapons of modern warfare encourage fighting at a distance wherein one does not see the adversary in flesh and blood, but the depersonalization is perpetuated, both consciously and unconsciously, by language:

> The Asians are "gooks" or "charlies," terms which immediately disqualify them as human beings who love, hate, live, hope, and die; no one really dies, but is "zapped," "wasted," or KIA—meaning killed in action. And there are no attacks or blood battles, there is merely "contact." There seem to be no words at all for danger, fear, horror, sadness, and so on; indeed, it all seemed to be a form of Newspeak.[14]

If the distancing of a man from his body and emotions is a crucial part of the violence seen in warfare, it is just as intimately connected to sexual violence against women. The two forms of violence have been connected since history began, for rape is part of warfare's ritual. The enemy must be humiliated by the abuse of "his" women. "In large measure, war is a form of sexual perversion."[15]

How can we understand the links between military violence and sexual violence against women? Obviously, war is the man's game. While women often nurture and support the warriors, it is difficult to find examples of matriarchal societies that have committed mass violence against other societies. Indeed, throughout history most societies have insisted that "manhood" be won by young males through rites of passage involving the willingness to endure and inflict violence—circumcision, hazing, beatings, killing wild animals or human enemies. One who fails the ordeal is less than a man. The warrior psyche can be achieved only by the systematic destruction of "feminine" characteristics in the young male. To feel neither emotion nor pain nor vulnerability is requisite. A blend of hostility toward women, repressed homosexual feeling, and phallic aggression is necessary for the manhood of the successful warrior. While men in battle grow to love each other, only the context of violence seems to justify any display of tenderness. "John Wayne can cradle a dying man in his arms, even shed a fugitive tear, but cannot touch another man in tenderness without raising the specter of being 'queer.' "[16]

Then, however, phallic aggression against women becomes an acceptable covering for unacceptable homosexual feelings. Gang rape becomes simply a "gang bang," a ritual of "real men." The penis, instead of an instrument of love, becomes a weapon: a tool, a rod, a gun. The soldier's understanding of his penis as a weapon is encouraged by the cadence many recruits learn in basic training, as I did. The drill instructor orders recruits to hold their rifles in one hand and their crotches in the other while yelling the cadence: "This is my rifle/This is my gun/This one's for fighting/This one's for fun!" Sam Keen's observation is soberingly accurate: "Once men have destroyed their own 'femininity' in order to mold themselves into warriors, they will inevitably perceive women as a subspecies of the enemy, a threat to their integrity, and will live with civil war within the self, the war between the sexes, and political war between nations. Those who live by the sword perceive all reality, inner and outer, through the metaphor of war."[17]

What of rape? Only in recent years has the message been clearly spoken: rape is a crime of violence, not an act of sexual lust.[18] For far too long we have been indoctrinated that in these "sex crimes" we are dealing with men who cannot sexually control themselves and with victims who really invite the rape. It is curious indeed that hierarchical sexual dualism assumes that *women* need sexual control, because their bodies and sensual natures are not really under the domination of a rational mind. But when it comes to rape we completely reverse the argument. Now it is men who cannot control their sexual passions.

Rape is a violent act of domination, of the male "keeping the woman in her place," of the control and punishment of women. In the rarer instances of male-male rape, humiliating a man by "womanizing" him is, in addition to the violation of the victim, another symbolic form of violence against women.

One rapist's testimony makes clear that the pleasure is not primarily genital, but that which comes from the sexual humiliation of the woman: "It was one of the most satisfying experiences I've ever had. I got more pleasure out of being aggressive, having power over her, her actions, her life. It gave me pleasure knowing there was nothing she could do. . . . My feelings were a mixture of sex and anger. I wanted pleasure, but I had to prove something, that I could dominate a woman. . . . The sex part wasn't very good at all."[19]

A dangerously false consciousness pervades our society about sexual violence. It is supported by a number of erroneous assumptions. The confusion holds that when an act using the sexual organs is performed, sexual pleasure is always the object. It is assumed that a man's sexual response is caused by an external source beyond his control, and hence the responsibility for an act lies with the victim, not the rapist. It is assumed that "romantic love" must involve a dominant-subordinate relationship. It is assumed that men have the right to impose their sexual acts upon others, without regard to the others' feelings or consent. It is assumed that a man's yes prevails over a woman's no. It is assumed that pleasure comes through overpowering another rather than sharing with another. It is assumed that the burden of proof lies with the victim, and that rape is primarily a woman's problem. It is assumed that violence is both acceptable and masculine. These destructive assumptions have become woven into much of our culture's definition of male sexuality.[20]

Rape is not inevitable. It is not programmed into male genes. It is a cultural variable. There are virtually rape-free societies like West Sumatra as well as rape-prone societies like ours. Anthropologist Peggy Reeves Sanday finds the incidence of rape lowest in those societies where physical and emotional nurturance is a strong reality and highest where masculinity is identified with an ideology of toughness and dominance. Rape, she concludes, is a form of concealing male vulnerability and dependency. It is the man's defense against his own despised "feminine dependencies," a defense he exercises by degrading and punishing the female body.[21]

The same dynamic seems to be present in male violence against those men who are presumed to be gay. The incidence of "queer bashing" and, indeed, murders of gay males by other males is tragically increasing with the AIDS epidemic. Here, again, is the anger of male vulnerability and dependency, now unleashed against those males who are assumed to violate the masculine norm and embody the feminine.

Sadly, much of the Bible provides little help in this matter. Violence against women frequently goes without condemnation. David weeps over the death of Amnon the rapist but does not weep for the victim, Tamar (2 Samuel 13). The daughter of Jephthah is sacrificed as part of a bargain for a military victory (Judges 11:29–40). The Levite's concubine is raped and killed to preserve a man's dignity (Judges 19). In addition to these scriptural problems concerning violence toward women, there are the sobering reminders of how biblical texts such as the Sodom and Gomorrah story for centuries have been wrenched out of their historical contexts and used to justify the persecution of gays.

Death and Bodily Change

Psychologically and spiritually, the connections between sexuality on the one hand and death and violence on the other are numerous and complex. Surely one connection lies in men's distance from their own body feelings. Another theme of the male sexual experience is important to recognize also: bodily change and vulnerability.

Unless men have coped with serious body-changing illness or accident, they simply have not experienced the amount of radical and repeated bodily changes common to women. The monthly menstrual cycle is a radical and repeated bodily change. And the experience is cyclical, not linear. It repeats itself over and over, introducing women in a dramatically immediate way to the cycles of nature, the changing seasons, the cycles of birthing and dying. Barren winter gives way to spring's fecundity.

Men tend to be more linear in their thinking. Straight lines move from here to there. They start somewhere and progress to a destination. Insofar as men's genitals are important to their self-images and values, this makes sense. Linearity is linked to the prized male erection. Here the straight line is the symbol of performance and success, of potency and of life itself. The repeating rhythms of cyclical experience are simply less part of the man's experience than the woman's. Further, those women who have experienced pregnancy, childbirth, and lactation know incredible body changing processes that men can never directly know. Whether menstruation or pregnancy and birth, these are processes over which the woman has little control: she can resist them or move with them, but such radical changes have their own momentum.

Death is the most profound bodily change of all. It is a change for which men are generally less prepared. It is the final challenge to linear thought, to onward-and-upward thinking. Death is the final question mark to every form of control, to every desire for mastery and winning. It is the final defeat of hardness and performance. In fact, it seems to be the defeat of all of the traditional masculine virtues and values. To those shaped to master life and overcome all obstacles, to those who dread anything connoting helplessness, to those accustomed to win, death is enemy. And we are not prepared for it. So Dylan Thomas says it for most men when he warns us not to go gentle into that good night. Rather, we should rage against the dying of the light.

The problem, of course, is that our male rage against death all too frequently becomes violence—violence which, paradoxically, nurtures the very thing it fears. The psychodynamics in sadomasochism (S&M) give us some clues as to why. Giving and receiving pain, both physical and emotional, as a means to sexual pleasure is largely a male phenomenon. Those women who participate as dominators typically are serving men's desires. Those men want to act out submissive roles. They want to be punished. And the exaggerated reversals of sex-role stereotypes in the dominance and submission aspects of S&M are played out in the rituals.

The desire for sadomasochistic expression seems to arise out of feelings of inner deadness. One psychiatrist has described the masochist this way: "[His] body is so contracted and the muscles of . . . [the] buttocks and pelvis are so tense that the sexual excitation does not get through to the genitals strongly enough. The beating, apart from its psychological meanings, breaks the tension and relaxes the muscles, allowing the sexual excitation to flow."[22] But this phenomenon is not limited to S&M practices. For the man who feels dead or powerless or impotent—in a whole variety of possible ways—violence (even experienced secondhand through the media) seems to tell him that he is alive.

The Confusing Issue of Masturbation

Most men somewhere in early adolescence received some threatening and erroneous messages about masturbation. One was disease—not just hair on your palms or green things growing out of your ears but weakness, depletion, and injury to your sexual powers. Granted, the extreme warnings were more typical of the late nineteenth-century medical hysteria about masturbation. To that era we are indebted for graham crackers and Kellogg's Corn Flakes, which were bland, non-sexually arousing, antimasturbatory foods invented for that purpose by Drs. Graham and Kellogg, respectively. Nevertheless, the fear of physical consequences has not entirely vanished. The

Boy Scout Manual on which I was reared and which went through fifty-seven printings said this: "[The male genitals are organs which] secrete into the blood material that makes a boy manly, strong, and noble. Any habit which a boy has that causes this fluid to be discharged from the body tends to weaken his strength, to make him less able to resist disease, and often unfortunately fastens upon him habits which later in life can be broken only with great difficulty."[23]

Still another warning to boys suggests that they have only a limited amount of semen programmed into their bodies for a lifetime, and it must not be depleted through "the solitary vice." Here is another version of the closed energy power system unfortunately typical of much male thinking: there is only a limited amount of power, and what one loses is gone forever. To complicate things, the depletion theory is frequently coupled with violent images: "You've only got so many bullets in your gun, buddy; don't shoot 'em off in the air—save 'em for the real thing." Now masturbation joins the limited power anxiety with the notion that male sexual powers are violent. After all, the boy learns that when he ejaculates, he "shoots off."

Other typical masturbation warnings more subtly but still effectively connect the boy's sexuality with violence. One warning is about the loss of manly self-control. From both the *Boy Scout Manual* and my father I got the message that masturbation is not necessary for "real men." A real man is disciplined, self-controlled, and saves himself for his future wife. To submit to one's own solitary pleasure is selfish and immature; sexual pleasure lies in another's power to give it to the self, and that other is a woman. But to the boy his body pleasure seems life-giving, a sense of his own goodness and worth. To defer this for years and to give a woman the key to his own sexual legitimation fosters resentment.

Now homophobic anxiety enters to complicate things. Since real men find sexual pleasure only in women, the continuing urge to masturbate must mean that the boy is attracted to the male body— his own. Thus the psychic anxieties of defending himself against homosexuality are attached to masturbation and become another source of resentment projected outward. However, in this instance the projection is aimed not only at homosexual males, who symbolize what the boy fears in himself, but also at women, who represent bodiliness itself.

Youthful masturbation anxieties and resentment of women can get all tangled together. Women are to be desired, but they also threaten males with depletion, loss of semen, loss of potency and power. They hold the key to unlock the male's legitimate sexual pleasure—and his pleasurable self-legitimation. They represent the other half of the mind-body split, the half of the self of which the boy has been deprived. They are the body and its feelings. The boy represents the mind, the will, the power of discipline. But it is the body that has sensations and pleasures and capacities to make one feel alive.

In adult life, it is the battering husband who is the extreme example of rage against a culture that keeps him trapped in half a human existence, an anger that encourages him to lash out against the woman who represents all the feelings of which he has been deprived. His rage against his own deadness turns to violence. Granted, the man who batters is the extreme case. Yet he represents that which most young males have been taught: a connection between sexual feelings, on the one hand, and resentment and violence, on the other. The possibility of masturbation or sexual self-pleasuring—potentially such a simple and benign source of self-affirmation at whatever age—has become entangled not only with feelings of guilt and anxiety but also with resentment about what the male has lost in a dualistic world.

No doubt, girls and women experience their own confusions around masturbation. In some ways, the experiences are similar, for women typically have been taught that men hold the keys to their sexual pleasure and legitimacy. Thus, some feminist women have affirmed the power of "liberating masturbation" as a way of claiming and owning their own bodies instead of submitting to their sexual ownership by men. Indeed, given the realities of patriarchy, this experience of sexual self-ownership would seem particularly important for women.

Nevertheless, it is still true that boys receive more antimasturbation exhortations. In spite of this, they begin to masturbate earlier and do it more frequently. The external location and ready availability of the male genitals are part of the story. The frequency, unpredictability, and attention-getting qualities of adolescent erections are also an explanation. But even more, it may be due to the boy's tendency to separate sexual feelings from emotional attachment, as we have observed earlier. Early in life boys have learned that sexual feelings have their own independence. Not so for the girl, for whom the explicitly sexual feelings were repressed in the early childhood experience with her mother. As Lillian Rubin remarks, "for a woman, sex usually has meaning only in a relational context—perhaps a clue to why so many girls never or rarely masturbate in adolescence or early adulthood."[24]

Yet my main concern here is not to compare the experiences of the two sexes. It is rather to explore the male's world. In this instance it is the concern to inquire about a question seldom asked: What does this extraordinarily common experience of masturbation mean to a boy's or man's inner life, to his ways of perceiving himself and his world? And, in the context of this chapter, what does it mean concerning his feelings about death and violence?

"I Believe in the Resurrection of the Body"

Several years ago my wife and I were on the Greek island of Santorini, reputed by tradition to be the Lost Atlantis, once submerged and later thrust up again above the sea by volcanic eruption. I reflected on that legend: how a whole people and their land, towns, and villages sank beneath the sea; how sailors reported hearing the tolling of bells from deep beneath the waters; how folk wondered how what was lost might be recovered.

I wonder the same about myself and my brothers. It is not so much that we must become something that we essentially are not. It is truer to say that we need to recover dimensions of ourselves that are really ours but which we have largely submerged. And many of us hear the tolling of the bells within us. What are those continents of our lives we need to recover?

The clues are similar to those we explored regarding the capacity for friendship. The Apostles' Creed affirms, "I believe in the resurrection of the body." In spite of our jogging and our Nautilus machines, we men have been more prone to body-spirit dualism than have women. To be proud of our bodies we will pummel them into shape. But we still tend to distance ourselves from the flesh that we are, treating the body as an "it," an instrument to be used.

The recovery of bodily connectedness, the recovery of the sense that we *are* our bodies, is the recovery of much that is vital in our faith tradition. It is the Hebraic sense of the self's unity as body-spirit. It is the erotic, incarnational reality of Christian revelation. It is the conviction that the Word continues to become flesh, and as flesh we are confirmed.

To recover the unity of the body-self and its eroticism is to recover more of our submerged capacities for feeling. When I am detached from my own bodily reality, I am also detached from the bodily reality of others. My abstractionism lures me into an exaggerated, often violent sense of reality. Think of medical care for the dying. Those who press for life extension at almost any cost typically are not the ones who are in close touch with the bodily reality of the dying patient. They are not usually those who have repeatedly bathed a fevered forehead or moistened parched lips. They are not the ones who hour after hour have caressed the body of their loved one and who viscerally know the awesome and awe-full difference between an intact higher brain function and a persistent vegetative state. When those things are not deeply known by being deeply felt, abstractions begin to take over, and the patient fades into a chart and a diagnosis. But to recover the body is to recover our connectedness with the bodily life of every other being.

To recover the body is to recover our capacity for pleasure, an important issue in violence. Considerable data now reveal the connections between these, and the extensive cross-cultural research of neurophysiologist James W. Prescott is a case in point. In society after society he discovered the close correlations between peacefulness and the experience of body pleasure, and between violence and the suppression of body pleasure. The positive connections were impressive: societies that are sex-positive and body-positive, and convey this to children through touch and physical nurturance, are demonstrably much more cooperative, peaceful societies. The same is true of individuals. The negative correlations also hold: pleasure-deprived youngsters are much more likely to become violent adults, and body-negative societies are predictably violent.[25] Body-selves deprived of pleasure become both angry and deadened. They search for violent ways of making themselves feel alive.

For the religiously sensitive, cultivating positive and pleasurable attitudes toward the body as a whole depends in no small measure on recovering the pleasure dimensions of our faith. Since the late Middle Ages, the Christian faith has largely lost its sense of the pleasure-loving God. Yet the Old Testament is replete with just this experience. The Hebrews knew the pleasuring God well. Thus the psalmist writes, "They feast on the bounty of your house, you give them drink from your river of pleasure" (Ps. 36:8, JB). And the lovers in the Song of Songs take delight in their holy, sensual play, reflecting the delight of their Creator. Nor is Jesus pictured as an ascetic, but as one who embraces the natural and the bodily. W. H. Auden observed, "As a rule it was the pleasure-haters who became unjust."[26] Indeed. Eros does not welcome a violent thanatos.

For men, to recover the body is to embrace less fearfully our finitude and mortality. In our dualistic theological heritage we have long had a theology of the *infinite*. We have lacked a theology of the *finite*.[27] Such a theology will affirm not only the glories and pleasures of our embodiment but also their pains, not just our fleshly ecstasies but also the burdens and tragedies that our flesh can become.

Our response to the AIDS crisis is a case in point. Both church and society have resisted facing the AIDS epidemic. The government spent more in a few weeks preparing for a swine flu epidemic that never materialized than it spent in the first four years of the AIDS epidemic. Religious institutions were notoriously slow to respond; we were several years into the epidemic before mainline denominations began to take initiatives.

The central problem is that AIDS brings together in one potent package the two greatest fears of our culture: sex and death. Now they have been united. Because of these deep fears, because of the already marginalized character of the disease's major victims, because of the ways in which this illness has been moralized, because of the extraordinarily complicated public policy issues—for all these reasons, in addition to the concrete suffering of countless people, AIDS is a major new challenge for us. And particularly for men, for we men have had great difficulties with sex and death.

As never before, we need incarnational spiritualities. Homophobia, the major stumbling block to our coping with AIDS, thrives on dualisms of disincarnation and abstraction that divide people from their bodily feelings and divide reality into two opposing camps. As never before, we need gracious spiritualities. Homophobia thrives on every theology of works justification, wherein persons must prove their worth and males must prove their manhood. As never before, we need erotic spiritualities. Homophobia thrives on erotophobia, the deep fear of sexuality and pleasure. It thrives in eros-deprived people because it grows in the resentments, the projections, and the anger of those whose own hungers go unmet. As never before, we need resurrection spiritualities. Homophobia thrives wherever there is fear of death, for then people try to dominate and control others in order to assure themselves of their own future. It thrives on bodily deadness, so deeply linked as it is with our sexual fears and repressions. The AIDS crisis is a major challenge to our sexual spirituality.

For men, to recover the body is to recover dependence and interdependence. As boys we learned in manifold ways that dependency was weak and unmanly. But the inability to affirm our dependency needs turns into violence. Our violence against nature tells this tale. René Descartes, the philosopher who laid much of the foundations for a mechanistic modern science, taught that the human body is simply a complicated machine. Western culture enthusiastically embraced Descartes's perceptions; they were important for the growing body of modern science and medicine in particular. But the ancient dualism was strongly reinforced. Once again the self became a spirit inhabiting a body, though now the body was seen as a complex and fascinating machine. From this viewpoint the biological nuts and bolts of that machine were studied, and the scientific grasp of the body's functions increased rapidly. But the unity of the self and the connectedness of the self to all else once again faded. Lost was the sense of human interdependence with the rest of creation. To Descartes the animals lacking the soul that animates the human body machine were *only* machines. And if just machines, animals could be treated with no more feeling than one treats a piece of metal.

I find far more wisdom in Chief Seattle. Over a century ago, when his tribe was forced to transfer its ancestral lands to the federal government, the Suquamish Indian chief said, "I will make one condition: the white man must treat the beasts of this land as his brothers and sisters. I am a savage and I do not understand any other way. I have seen a thousand rotting buffaloes on the prairie, left by the white man who shot them from a passing train. I am a savage and do not understand how the smoking iron horse can be more important than the buffalo we kill only to stay alive. Every part of this earth is sacred to my people. Every shining pine needle . . . every mist in the dark woods . . . every humming insect. . . . The sap which courses through the trees carries the memories of the red [people]. . . . This shining water that moves in the streams and rivers is not just water but the blood of our ancestors."[28] That is the wisdom of the body.

Male recovery of bodily life means the recovery of a sense of the cyclical. We men cannot literally experience the biological cycle in the way that women know it. They know the possibility of allying themselves with the natural flow of life's energies. Our male body experience is more linear. But we are not simply biologically determined. The linear has its marvelous gifts and strengths for individual and social life, but when it is absolutized as the only correct perception, we all suffer.

No longer can we males pretend that our perception is the entire human perception. No longer can we assume that history is always more important than nature, that Jacob's ladder is more adequate than Sarah's circle. And when we come to that realization—even though menstruation, childbirth, and menopause are not our immediate experience—we sense a new connectedness with our own selves and with the whole of nature. We begin to accept the seasonal nature of life, and with it accept death—not as a defeat but as a fitting and proper destiny for human beings. That does not mean we ought to enjoy dying. We perhaps did not enjoy being born, either. But both were and are part of our destined cycle, something we can affirm.[29]

Men's recovery of the body has something to do with the recovery of a resurrection faith. "I believe in the resurrection of the body and the life everlasting." What that means, who can adequately say? However inadequately, I think we can say at least this. It does not mean any literal resuscitation of corpses. It does mean that our bodily life, our *sexual* bodily life, is intrinsically part of us and is valued eternally by God, the Cosmic Lover.

If Otto Rank and Ernest Becker are right, the sexual experience itself predictably arouses death anxieties. For in sex our animal natures become more evident to us, and as animals we are clearly mortal. Moreover, in the sex act at the peak of pleasure we seem to lose our sense of individuation and distinctness. That in some dim way is the threat of death. Not without reason have the French called orgasm "the little death." Rank and Becker have both argued that it is anxiety about death that makes us flee from our bodies.[30] At the same time our sexual experience prepares us for a resurrection faith. At its best, our sexual loving provides clues to a reality beyond that which we experience. "What it evokes in us, human love and desire cannot fulfill. It requires God for completion."[31]

The self's inner dialogue goes both ways—from our sexuality to our spirituality, and the other direction as well. Just as our sexual experience evokes in us an intimation of that beyond what we now know, so also resurrection faith enhances and interprets our sexuality. It just may be that the affirmation of the resurrection faith might free us more fully to enjoy our fragile, limited, and delicious mortality. As a male, I can begin to affirm my passive and receptive side. I can affirm that controlling and winning are not always my prerogatives, and surely I will not conquer death by these means.

H. Richard Niebuhr once observed that the great religions of the world made their most decisive impacts upon human behavior not by teaching people new rules and moral laws but by changing their images of time.[32] In the symbol of resurrection, Christian faith has tried to say something about the meaning of time. It seems to say that there is a capacity to be "at home" in this mortal life precisely because what we see and know here and now is not the final answer.

When we live as if death were the final meaning to it all, we inevitably cultivate "an ethics of death." There are many kinds. One is "Eat, drink, and be merry, for tomorrow we die." Another is seeing life as a personal survival trip: if I don't look out for me, no one else will. Indeed, every sort of survival ethics is an ethics of death, to which an insane nuclear arms race is grimly eloquent testimony. An ethics of death based upon survival is an ethics of fear. It is an attempt to grasp, to possess, to control, because the future is so uncertain. But when one begins to live with an ultimate image of resurrection time instead of dying time, something begins to happen. Niebuhr put it in words one can hardly improve: "Once we were blind in our distrust of being: now we begin to see. We were aliens and alienated in a strange, empty world: now we begin sometimes to feel at home. We were in love with ourselves and all our little cities: now we are falling in love, we think, with being itself."[33]

FIVE
Embracing Masculinity

Masculinity: Images and Tales

Men who are aware of the destructiveness of machismo and sensitive to the feminist critique have engaged in considerable reexamination of traditional models of masculinity in recent years. Mark Gerzon's *A Choice of Heroes* is a good example.[1] The author finds five images of masculinity lodged deep within our social consciousness. These models exist because they once seemed useful, promising both survival and well-being. Now they have become destructive and require alternatives. What are they?

The Frontiersman is the quick-fisted white male loner conquering the frontier—Daniel Boone, Kit Carson, Davy Crockett. His enemies were untamed nature, the outlaw, and the savage redskin. Conquest, especially conquest of the wilderness, was the key. The land was a virgin "she," and every real man wanted a piece. In place of this rapacious understanding, Gerzon commends a new image, the Healer. Here is the man with a different view both of himself and of the land, a man aware of the need for healing the environment.

The Soldier is the defender image. Strong and courageous, he armors his body and emotions. He represses his feelings of vulnerability, his fears, and his sensitivities in order to be ready for necessary violence. His sexuality itself becomes an instrument of aggression, and his penis is a weapon. An alternative model for the new man is the Mediator. Literally the word comes from *mediare*, "to stand in the middle." This man insists neither that life be a battle nor that heroism be equated with fighting. Rather, his goal is that adversaries coexist peacefully and cooperate if possible.

The Breadwinner is the head of his family and responsible for its economic support. Here is the patriarchal family, with a public man and a private woman, an absent father and a nurturing mother. The breadwinner's ethic is work and success. His manhood is established by the size of his paycheck. An alternative image is that of the Companion. The word, composed of *com* (together) and *panis* (bread), literally suggests one who eats with another. The daily bread is not won by the man and given to the other, but made and eaten together. Life is shared.

The Expert, another traditional image, is the man who possesses knowledge and hence is in control. He is more concerned with establishing and maintaining his power than he is with furthering the truth. Knowledge is power and a means of control. A better image is the Colleague. Again, a composite word, it comes from the verb meaning literally "to choose together." The colleague respects competence and expertise but knows that its value lies in sharing. He is the enemy of unnecessary hierarchies, the champion of shared power and leadership.

Finally, the Lord bears the image of the soul. Since the maker of heaven and earth is presumably male, every man is flattered to be in "His" image. The feminine in the divine is denied and repressed, hence also the feminine in the man. God is male, and male is god. The needed new image is the Nurturer. Such a man does not feign omniscience, nor does he lord it over others. He does not presume to save others but to join them in mutual empowerment.

I find Gerzon's analysis helpful and constructive. Significantly, he has taken the feminist critique of distorted masculinism seriously, and his alternative images are desperately needed. Yet, as he says in conclusion, these emerging masculinities—Healer, Mediator, Companion, Colleague, Nurturer—have a striking similarity. "The human qualities they symbolize transcend sexual identity. They reflect awareness of the earth, of work and family, and of the human body, mind, and soul, an awareness that any man or woman can develop. . . . Unlike the old archetypes, which were for men only, the emerging masculinities are not. They are, in fact, emerging *humanities.*"[2]

In other words, while there are distinctive and identifiable traits connected with false or distorted masculinism, there is nothing distinctive about a man's experience *as a man* that provides a grounding for a constructive male identity (or, presumably, about a woman's experience as woman for hers). "Masculinity" and "femininity" are simply interchangeable names for a new "humanity." Gerzon is not alone in that conviction. Many advocates of androgyny would agree.

However, other men who are equally serious about naming and realizing new nonpatriarchal identities are not so sure. I am one of them. Is there not something good, important, *and distinctive* about the experience of maleness itself? Something that can produce an

energy which is not oppressive but rather creative and life-giving—
and recognizably male? A "deep masculine" that men can find in
themselves and justly celebrate?

The remarkable attention given to one particular article in recent
years suggests that many men are asking these questions. The article,
"The Meaning of Being Male," is an interview with poet Robert Bly.
Before the rise of feminist consciousness, according to the poet, the
image of the male in our society had massive inadequacies. It was a
fairly clear vision—aggressive, hardworking, emotionally unexpres-
sive, athletic, and patriotic. But it was unbalanced. It was deficient
in feminine space. It lacked compassion. Then men began to pay
attention to the development of their own feminine side. Now, however, there is something wrong:

> The male in the past twenty years has become more thoughtful, more
> gentle. But by this process he has *not* become more free. . . . I see the
> phenomenon of what I would call the "soft male" all over the country
> today. . . . They're lovely, valuable people—I like them—and they're
> not interested in harming the earth or starting wars or working for
> corporations. There's something favorable toward life in their whole
> general mood and style of living. But something's wrong. Many of
> these men are unhappy: there's not much energy in them. They are
> life-preserving but not exactly *life-giving.* [3]

Bly then turns to the Grimms' tale of "Iron John." Here is the
scenario: Near the castle, people are strangely disappearing in the
forest. One day an unknown hunter shows up at the castle looking
for work and volunteers to investigate the mystery. He goes into the
forest with his dog, and as they are walking by a pond a large hand
comes out of the water, grabs the dog, and pulls it down. The hunter,
not wanting to abandon his dog and yet being a sensible man, returns
to the castle and recruits other men to help him. Together they go
back with buckets to drain the pond. Lying at the bottom is a big
man covered with reddish hair, the color of rusty iron. They capture
him and take him back to the castle, where the king has him placed
in a cage in the courtyard.

Interrupting the story, Bly interprets. When the male looks into
his psyche, beyond his feminine side to the dark bottom of his deep
pool, he finds an ancient male covered with hair, symbolic of the
instinctive, the sexual, and the primitive. Though they have begun
to explore underdeveloped feminine sides of themselves, making contact with this "wild man" is a process many men yearn for but have
not explored.

The story continues. One day the eight-year-old prince is playing
in the courtyard with his beloved golden ball. The ball rolls into the

cage, and the wild man grabs it. Iron John will return the ball only if the prince will release him from the cage, and the wild man knows that the key to the lock is under the queen's pillow. Since his parents are away and since he wants the ball so badly, the prince fetches the key and opens the cage. As Iron John begins to leave, the prince, fearing his parents' anger, calls to him for help. The wild man hoists the boy onto his shoulders and they go off into the forest together, where the prince will learn about his manhood.

Bly observes that the recurrent fairy-tale image of the golden ball suggests wholeness, the unity of personality, the sense of connectedness with the universe. Like the sun, it gives a radiant energy from within. Further, that deep, nourishing spiritual energy for the male lies in the *deep* masculine, under the water. It is not the shallow, macho, snowmobile masculine. It is wet, dark, and low. It is something a woman cannot give to a man (nor can he give her what is distinctively her energy). It has to be appropriated slowly and resolutely, bucket by bucket, with the help of other men. It is something like that which the Greeks called Zeus energy: intelligence, health, compassion, robustness, and positive power in the service of community. It is the "moist male" and a religious dimension of maleness.[4]

The use of fairy and folk tales to examine the meanings of our gender images and possibilities is fairly common. Understandably, many women have taken strong issue with the images in "Cinderella" and "Sleeping Beauty."[5] Here is the passive woman, awaiting rescue or awakening by the dashing male hero. Such tales from the patriarchal past do gross injustice to women, and their male images are of little help to men. It is useful, however, to turn to one other fairy tale to locate some problems involved in recovering the masculine energy.

The story is *Pinocchio.*[6] Gepetto has shaped Pinocchio's body from a piece of unusual wood. Though the wood itself is already animated, the puppet remains a puppet until the fairy godmother's touch brings him to life. This is a common perception of many a young man. His breadwinner father has provided for the material aspects of his life. But his father's passions have been invested at work, and there is little left at home to give life to the son. The son lacks the manhood that must come from men. His life feels as though it has been given largely through a woman's touch, his mother's. But that life still lacks something, a masculine energy that he now seeks.

The tale suggests another theme, the body. Though Pinocchio has been given life by the woman's touch, most of his body does not truly seem alive. Only one part does, and that one has a mind of its own. Whenever Pinocchio lies, that organ conspicuously enlarges and sticks out in front of him, much to his embarrassment. We might take the lie that causes his nose to grow as a simile for the lie that men continue to believe about their bodies. The lie is that a man's body is largely lifeless except for one organ, which has the capacity to grow larger on particular occasions, and sexual energy is confined to that organ.

Pinocchio raises important questions. Is there anything authentically male about men, independent of women's contribution, that is important to their masculine identity? And, what is the place, if any, of that age-old emblem of manhood, the male genitals? Let us look at masculinity through this particular lens.

Body Theology and Male Genitals

What are the spiritual meanings of the male genitals? The question seldom has been asked, particularly in Christian conversation and literature. There are predictable and important questions about the appropriateness of even considering the issue. Before we go further, we must attend to them.

First, some will simply find the question distasteful. Anti-body feelings nurtured by centuries of sexual dualism are strong indeed. And the genitals are the supreme test. Discomfort over seriously considering the body to be of spiritual significance becomes repulsion when the focus is the genitals. The reaction is predictable, but deeply regrettable. God has created us good in all our parts, and an incarnationalist faith bids us celebrate *all* of the body as vehicle of divine presence and meaning.

Can the sexual feelings, functions, and meanings of our genitals be important modes of revelation? Admittedly, the thought has been far from commonplace in Christian theology. Yet a broader view is needed. The distinguished historian of religion Mircea Eliade saw our human sexual experience as an "autonomous mode of cognition." It is, he believed, a fundamental way of knowing reality immediately and directly. Eliade went so far as to declare that sexuality's "primary and perhaps supreme valency is the cosmological function. . . . Except in the modern world, sexuality has everywhere and always been a hierophany, and the sexual act an integral action and therefore also a means of knowledge."[7] Sexuality thus is a pathway into the mystery of the cosmos. As a hierophany it is a manifestation of the sacred, revealing to us what is beyond our conscious rational apprehension. True, this is a bold claim that goes against the accepted view. Centuries of dualism have taught us that the body (especially in its sexual dimensions) reveals nothing of the spirit. But a holistic spirituality demands that we make this bold claim.

Even if this is granted, however, some will object that such a focus for the masculinity question will simply invite back all the distortions of genitalized masculinity. I am sympathetic with this concern. Such distortions are prevalent in men's experience, and they are serious. Let us name them once more. There is the genitalization of sexual feeling, the Pinocchio-like experience of life in the one organ while the rest of the body feels lifeless and deprived of eros. The consequences are manifold, and we have already examined some of them. There is the one-sided phallic interpretation of reality, which overvalues the linear, the vertical, and the hard while undervaluing the cyclical, the horizontal, and the soft. Again, the results in men's one-sided shaping of their world are enormous. Also, there are the ways in which the penis becomes associated with violent and detached meanings, as its slang names amply suggest—cock, prick, tool, rod, and even a gun with its bullets. Such meanings do not readily suggest the genitals as graciously integrated into the body of love. And there are body-affirming feminists, men as well as women, who will resist the thought of *any* kind of male genital affirmation precisely because they are so keenly aware of the wounds caused by phallic violence. Attention of any kind given to the penis might suggest just another thinly disguised form of masculinist oppression. These suspicions, sadly enough, are understandable.

Where are we left? One option seems to be the firm discipline of the genitals. If my penis seems to have a mind of its own, I must deprive it of that freedom. I will be its master and keep it from running amok. The trouble with servants and slaves, however, is that they seldom know their place. They are treated as machines, whose only purpose is to perform the functions determined by their masters. But either as slave or as machine, that part of me will be dead. I will have deprived it of its right to live *except* as slave or machine. This puts me right back into the dualism of control: the higher over the lower, master over servant. The spirit or mind with its higher capacities for thought and virtue must control the body, especially the penis, with its physical appetites.

Even though many Christians seem to hold a different theological theory about the body in all of its parts—good because made by God, and a temple of the Holy Spirit—a simple test proposed by H. A. Williams suggests another reality.[8] Suppose that in church on Sunday morning this lesson from Paul is read: "I appeal to you therefore, ... by the mercies of God, to present your bodies as a living sacrifice, holy and acceptable to God, which is your spiritual worship" (Rom. 12:1). What prospects come into our imaginations as response to this exhortation? Does it conjure up images of physical pleasure and ecstasy? "Not at all," says Williams. "The prospect conjured up is the dreary duty of controlling the body, or if the body is recalcitrant of forcing it, negatively, not to do this, that, or the other, and positively to energize itself in the performance of this or the other kind of good works. But whether understood negatively or positively the exhortation is taken automatically as a call to the joyless task of disciplining the body and oppressing it by imposing upon it an alien will, treating it in short as a dead object to be pushed around."[9] If that is true of our actual functioning attitudes toward the body as a whole (regardless of the theological notions we might have in our heads), how much truer it probably is of our genitals.

However, the master-slave discipline of the genitals will not work. They are finally treated not as a vital part of us but as something denied the right to live except as slave machines. Nor will it work to ignore our genitals or consign them to hell as beyond redemption. It will not work because that which is consigned to hell just will not lie down. While Williams is speaking of bodies in general, his words are just as true of our genitals in particular: "Being in hell, the place of the undead, they are always somehow planning and threatening their revenge, and they may in the end catapult us into nuclear catastrophe. . . . The body deprived of *eros* inevitably becomes the champion of *thanatos*. Better to die completely than to fester in hell."[10] Indeed, hell is the place of the dead who will not accept their death.

The alternative, however, is not to give our genitals the freedom of their demands. That was the solution for some people in the "sexual revolution" of recent decades: if in the past we have oppressed our bodies and genitals, let us now give the slaves their freedom. But subjecting our genitals to oppression has made them subject to compulsions, and compulsions do not satisfy. They give only fleeting, momentary relief. Compulsions of genital instinct just replace compulsions of the head, but there still is no fulfillment. We still remain divided. Only the balance of power has changed. What we need is truly the resurrection of the body in all its parts. We do not need the crazy behavior of the slave let loose for the evening.

Still, we cannot insist on utter clarity or purity in our experience. Williams's words are wise: "For in experience compulsion and resurrection are often mixed up together. Indeed the experience of resurrection often grows from what was originally an experience of compulsion. If we are perfectionists or purists here we shall find ourselves cut off from all experience of love."[11] Sometimes illusion is the midwife of reality, and paralysis from the fear of illusion may mean that reality will forever escape us.

In recent years a number of feminist women have fruitfully explored the spiritual meanings of their own female body experiences—

the nature of their breasts and genitals, their experiences of menstruation and birthing. We men traditionally have identified women with their biology and neglected our own. It is time that we inquire about ourselves.

Phallus

In his suggestive book *Phallos: Sacred Image of the Masculine,* Eugene Monick explores the psychic and religious dimensions of the male experience of his phallus, his erect penis.[12] Every male, he asserts, directly knows the meanings of erection: strength, hardness, determination, sinew, straightforwardness, penetration. Because erection is not fully under a man's conscious control, because the penis seems to decide on its own when, where, and with whom it wants erection and action, the phallus seems to be an appropriate metaphor for the masculine unconscious.

From time immemorial it has fascinated men. Numerous ancient expressions of phallic art and worship are well known, from the common representations on ancient Greek pottery, to the huge erection of the Cerne giant (carved in the first century B.C. by the Celts into a chalk hill in Dorset, England), to the modern-day Hindu cult of Shiva, where the phallus is an image of divinity.[13] Beyond such outward evidences of religious veneration, men of every time and place have known a religious quality to their phallic experience. To adapt Rudolf Otto's words, it is the *mysterium tremendum.* Such encounters with the numinous produces responses of fascination, awe, energy, and a sense of the "wholly other."[14] Through the phallus, men sense a resurrection, the capacity of the male member to return to life again and again after depletion. An erection makes a boy feel like a man and makes a man feel alive. It brings the assurance and substantiation of masculine strength.

Yet, as with other experiences of the holy, males feel ambivalent about the phallus. Erections must be hidden from general view. They are an embarrassment when they occur publicly. Men joke about erections with each other but cannot speak seriously. The secret is exposed only with another person in intimacy or when a male permits himself to experience his potency alone. If the mystery is exposed publicly, somehow the sacred has been profaned.

Furthermore, there is a double-sidedness to the phallic experience. One dimension is the *earthy* phallus.[15] This is the erection perceived as sweaty, hairy, throbbing, wet, animal sexuality. In some measure it is Bly's Iron John maleness. Men who have rejected this may be nice and gentle, but they seem to lack life-giving energy. Their keys remain hidden under the queen's pillow—indeed, with the cooperation of the king, for the powers of social order always distrust the earthy phallus. And there is reason for distrust, because there can be an ugly, brutal side to the earthy phallus that uses others for gratification when this part of a man's sexuality does not find balance with other sides. Yet without the positive presence of earthy energy a man is bland. There is gentleness without strength, peacefulness without vitality, tranquility without vibrancy.

Men also experience the *solar* phallus.[16] Solar (from the sun) means enlightenment. A man's erect penis represents to him all that stands tall. It is proud. The solar experience of erection puts a man in touch with the excitement of strenuous achievement. It is the Jacob's ladder and the mountain climb, which rise above the earthy and the earthly. It is the satisfaction of straining to go farther intellectually, physically, and socially. Solar phallus is transcendence. It is the church steeples and skyscrapers that men are inclined to build. Solar phallus represents what most men would like to have noted in their obituaries. In Carl Jung's thinking, solar phallus is the very substance of masculinity It is, he believed, *logos,* which transforms thought into word, just as eros (which he called feminine) transforms feeling into relatedness. I believe Jung misled us with his bifurcations of masculine and feminine principles, unfortunately grounding them in common gender stereotypes. Nevertheless, logos is an important part of the male experience both represented and invited by the solar phallus.

As with the earthy phallus, there is a shadow side to the experience of the solar phallus, too. It is the patriarchal oppression of those who do not "measure up." It is proving one's worth through institutional accomplishments. It is the illusion of strength and power that comes from position. It is the use of technical knowledge to dominate. It is political power which defends its ideological purity at virtually any price and then prides itself on standing tall in the saddle. It is addiction to the notion that bigger is better. The distortions of solar phallus are legion. Yet without its integrated positive energy, a man lacks direction and movement. Without the urge to extend himself, he is content with the mediocre. Without the experience of the wholly other, life loses its self-transcendence.

Thus far I have agreed in broad outline with Monick's significant analysis: the importance of both the earthy and the solar phallus, their integration, and the dangers of their shadow sides. Here, however, Monick stops. He believes that phallus, the erect penis, is *the* sacred image of the masculine. That seems to be enough. But it is not. Left there, I fear we are left with priapism.

In Roman mythology Priapus, son of Dionysus and Aphrodite, was the god of fertility. His usual representations were marked both by grotesque ugliness and an enormous erection. In human sexual disorders, priapism is the painful clinical condition of an erection that will not go down. Priapus and priapism are symbolic of the idolatry of the half-truth. Phallus, the erection, indeed is a vital part of the male's experience of his sexual organs. Hence, it is usually a vital part of his spirituality. But it is only part. Were it the whole thing, his sexuality and his spirituality would be painful and bizarre, both to himself and to others. That this in fact is too frequently the case is difficult to deny. Our phallic experience gives vital energy, both earthy and solar. But we also need the affirmative experience of the *penis.*

Penis

In our daily lives, almost all men are genitally soft by far the greater share of the time. Genitally speaking, penis rather than phallus is our awareness, insofar as we are aware at all. (For economy in words, I will use "penis" for the organ in its flaccid, unaroused state.) We are genitally limp most of our waking moments, and while erections come frequently during sleep we are seldom aware of them.

Psychically, the experiences of phallus and of penis seem very different. An erection during waking hours claims my attention. Frequently I choose not to act upon its aroused urgency, and sometimes in embarrassment I hide its evidence. But its claims on my psychic awareness have an undeniable phallic imperiousness. The penis is different. Most of the time I am unaware of it. It is just there, part of me, functioning in my occasional need to urinate, but most often invisible from my conscious awareness, much as an internal organ. But when I am conscious of it in dressing or undressing, I am aware of its difference from phallus. Penis is considerably smaller. It is wrinkled. There is even something comical about the contrast (as a man's wife or lover occasionally might tell him). It has a relaxed humility. In its external existence it seems vulnerable, and with the testicles it needs jockstrap protection during the body's vigorous athletics.

In spite of the quantitative dominance of penis time, men tend to undervalue penis and overvalue phallus. Part of that, indeed, simply stems from conscious awareness. When the phallus is present, it demands our attention. The penis does not. Part of the difference, however, is a matter of intentional valuation. We have been taught and have learned to value phallic meanings in patriarchy: bigger is better (in bodily height, in paychecks, in the size of one's corporation or farm); hardness is superior to softness (in one's muscles, in one's facts, in one's foreign policy positions); upness is better than downness (in one's career path, in one's computer, in one's approach to life's problems). In "a man's world," small, soft, and down pale beside big, hard, and up.

Penis is undervalued, also, because we so commonly identify male energy and true masculinity with the vitality of young manhood. Infant males and little boys have frequent erections, but true phallus—the heroic sword raised on high—is the property of young manhood. As age comes upon a man, hardness changes and modifies. It is less apparent, less urgent, less the signature of his body. Phallus bears intimations of life and vigor, while penis bears intimations of mortality. Fearing mortality, men tend to reject the qualities of penis and project them upon women who are then seen to be small, soft, and vulnerable, qualities inferior to the phallic standard. Wrinkles, so typical of penis, are not permitted in women if they are to retain their womanly attraction.[17]

But the undervaluing of penis and the overvaluing of phallus take their toll. The price is paid by all who suffer because of patriarchy, for this spiritual body dynamic, while hardly the sole cause of such oppression, surely contributes to it. But oppressors themselves are also oppressed in the process. So what is the price paid by men? One cost we must look at is the deprivation of a significant kind of masculine spiritual energy and power.

The history of western spirituality reveals two traditional paths to the presence of God: the Via Positiva and the Via Negativa, the positive way and the negative way.[18] The former is a way of affirmation, of thanksgiving, of ecstasy. It is the way of light, the way of being filled by the sacred fullness and rising to the divine height. The Via Negativa is a way of emptying and being emptied. It is the way of darkness. It is sinking into nothingness and into the sacred depths. In spirituality, each way needs the other for balance and completion. The overdevelopment of one to the detriment of the other brings distortion. I believe that in the male experience the Via Positiva has profound associations with the phallus, while the Via Negativa correspondingly is connected to the penis. And in most men it is the latter which remains underrecognized, underclaimed, underaffirmed.

Consider some aspects of the Via Negativa as expressed by a great Christian mystic who knew this way, Meister Eckhart (1260–1327). It is quiet, not active: "Nothing in all creation is so like God as stillness." It is the darkness more than the light: "The ground of the soul is dark." It appears to be less rather than more: "God is not found in the soul by adding anything but by a process of subtraction." It is a deep sinking and a letting go: "We are to sink eternally from letting go to letting go into God." It is the abandoning of focus and attention: "One should love God mindlessly, without mind or mental activities or images or representations." It is the paradox of nothingness embracing something: "God is a being beyond being and a nothingness beyond being. . . . God is nothingness. And yet God is something."[19]

All such modes of the Via Negativa are a man's experiences of his penis, not his phallus. Think of sinking and emptying. The penis is empty of the engorging blood that brings hard excitement to the phallus. Its flaccidity is a letting go of all urgency. It has nowhere to go. It just is. It just hangs and sinks between the legs.

Sinking, emptying, is a way of spirituality.[20] It means trusting God that we do not need to *do,* that our *being* is enough. It means yielding to our tears that keep coming and coming once they begin. It means trusting ourselves to the darkness of sleep, so like the darkness of death. It means abandoning our own achievements and resting in the depths of meaning we do not create. Men often resist these things. But sinking and emptying are as necessary to the spirit's rhythms as they are to the genitals'. Without periods of genital rest, a man lacks phallic capacity. Without times of retreat to the desert, there is no energy for greening.

Or consider darkness, another theme of the Negativa. It seems related to the cosmic womb of our origins, and it has its own energy. Rainer Maria Rilke writes, "You darkness, that I come from/I love you more than all the fires that fence in the world . . . and it is possible a great energy is moving near me/I have faith in nights."[21] But most men are less at home in the darkness than in the light. We are heirs of the Enlightenment, a male-oriented rational movement that sought to shed light on everything. Our psyches seem to link darkness with death, and fear of death is characteristic of the patriarchal society. Starhawk, speaking of the holiness of darkness, maintains that the dark is "all that we are afraid of, all that we don't want to see—fear, anger, sex, grief, death, the unknown."[22]

The penis, in contrast to the phallus, is a creature of the dark. It is resting. Asleep. Usually we are unaware of its presence. But we are conscious of the presence of phallus, just as we are aware of the presence of light. Taught to prize light and fear the dark, we have also been taught to prize the phallic virtues and to fear the meanings of penis. Its quiescence seems symbolic of death, its limpness the reminder of male-dreaded impotence, and fears of death and impotence are the cause of much destruction. But without the darkness there is no growth, no mystery, no receptivity, no deep creativity. Without the gentle dark, light becomes harsh.

Masculine Energy: Beyond Androgyny

For a variety of reasons, men have come to believe that phallus is the emblem of masculinity, the signature of true maleness. But this is only partly true, and partial truths taken as the whole truth become both demonic and self-destructive. A man's penis is as genuinely his reality as is his phallus, and just as important to his male humanity. Spiritually, the Via Negativa is as vital to him as the Via Positiva. It may also be the case that men's overvaluation of phallus, and the undervaluation of penis, is one important reason for our confusions about gender identities and the notion of androgyny.

The concept of androgyny has been commonplace for some years.[23] Most simply put, it denotes the integration within a single person of traits traditionally identified by gender stereotypes as masculine and as feminine. Thus, androgynous people characterize themselves both as strongly self-reliant, assertive, and independent, and as strongly understanding, affectionate, and compassionate. Androgyny is an appealing alternative to the oppressiveness of gender role stereotypes. It goes beyond the false dualism of the belief that there are certain inherent personality traits of the male and of the female. It moves us beyond oppressive gender expectations into the possibility of a more genuinely human liberation for each and for all.

The concept seems appealing theologically. Nicolas Berdiaev, the Russian philosopher-theologian, pressed the idea in 1914, long before its currency in social psychology. There is, he declared, a fundamental androgyny of the human being created in the image of God, an androgyny that the gender roles of the world have not destroyed. "In fact, 'in the beginning' it is neither man nor woman who bears the divine similitude. In the beginning it is only the androgyne . . . who bears it. The differentiation of the sexes is a consequence of the fall of Adam." Now, estranged from our essence, we have a compelling desire to recover our lost unity through recovery of the lost principle. "It is by means of this femininity that the male-human can once again be integrated to the androgynous source of his nature, just as it is through this masculine principle that the female-human can be . . . integrated to her lost androgynous source. . . . Ultimately it is in God that the lover meets with the beloved, because it is in God that personality is rooted. And the personality in God, in its original state, is androgynous."[24]

Berdiaev was ahead of his time. Most later male theologians of this century have not seriously raised the androgynous theme but rather have emphasized the need of gender complementarity. Karl Barth is typical.[25] He believes that our humanity, created in the image of God, is "fellow-humanity." We are incomplete by ourselves. Men and women come into their fullness only in intimate relation to persons of the opposite sex. Barth's position rests on the assumption that by nature the personalities and qualities of the two sexes are essentially different and that each needs the other for completion. There is no androgyny. Barth draws a clear conclusion from this concerning homosexuality: it is perversion and idolatry. One who seeks same-sex union is narcissistically seeking the self. It is a quest for self-satisfaction and self-sufficiency, but such aims can never be realized because the two sexes are fundamentally necessary for each other. While I find Barth's emphasis on the *social* nature of our true humanity commendable, his notion of gender complementarity is deeply flawed. It rests on the uncritical use of gender stereotypes, and it particularly oppresses gays and lesbians, all who are female (because those stereotypes do), and all who are single (among the latter, Jesus included). The notion of gender complementarity is a giant step backward from androgyny.

Androgyny is an ancient theme, prevalent in classical mythology. In Christian thought it was present far earlier than Berdiaev. Yet I believe his was the first clear statement of the essential androgyny of *both* sexes. Earlier versions, blatantly patriarchal, found only the male androgynous. Woman was made necessary as a differentiated sexual being only because man had lost his state of perfection and needed her feminine principle for his human completion. She, however, remained half human.

Nevertheless, androgyny as a theological concept, even in Berdiaev's promising way, runs into some of the same problems as are present in current social psychology. One problem is both definitional and practical. Does the concept mean that both "feminine" and "masculine" characteristics somehow essentially (by nature or by God's design) exist together in every individual, and thus they should be developed and expressed? This seems to be the most common understanding. In the psychological literature sometimes it is labeled "monoandrogynism," to distinguish it from variations of the theme. But this can be oppressive in its own way. Now each person has two sets of gender traits to learn and incorporate instead of one. Now everyone is expected to acquire thoroughly both "instrumental/agentic" ("masculine") and "expressive/nurturant" ("feminine") characteristics in equal amounts, a standard that would seem to double the pressure that people traditionally have felt.

Even more basically, another problem is that androgyny is based on the assumption that there are, indeed, two distinct and primordial sets of personality characteristics—one "masculine," the other "feminine." Even if we assume that each sex is capable of developing both sets of traits, the definition itself perpetuates the very problem it had hoped to overcome. It still locates one constellation of qualities essentially and dominantly in men and the other constellation essentially and dominantly in women. Jung's psychological thought exemplifies this, as do those who draw upon him, for example, in speaking of the male's need to develop "his latent feminine side." In fact, there is a built-in obsolescence to this concept. For if each sex stopped adhering only to its primary characteristics, and if the two gender stereotypes subsequently became less distinct from each other, androgyny in the current sense would lose its meaning.

One way out of the conceptual difficulty is simply to envision the complete transcendence of gender-role traits (sometimes called the "polyandrogynous" possibility). Here, personality traits are seen as having no connection at all with biological sex. Each individual is viewed as different from every other individual, for each has unique interests and capacities. In many ways this vision is promising. It frees individuals to be who they uniquely are. However, there remains a problem. The notion of gender-role transcendence, while it honors uniqueness, does not hold up any vision of inclusiveness or relative balance in personal qualities. A given individual could still be as one-sided as ever, even though the rigid linkage between certain traits and one's biological sex had been severed.

Nevertheless, an important question still remains. Is there anything *distinctive* to the experience of one's own biological sex that grounds us in the development of a more whole personality, a personhood richer than its specific gender stereotype? More particularly, is there anything in the male body experience that enables him to transcend the traditional cultural images of masculinity?

If that *is* the case, it is difficult to see why the call to more inclusive personhood would be fundamentally oppressive. If as a man I were called upon to acquire feminine qualities *in addition to my natural masculinity,* that would be one thing. I might be capable of doing that, but it would feel much like learning a second language as an adult, adding another linguistic capability to my native tongue. Even if through years of study and practice I become somewhat proficient, my second language would always be that—a second language, added on, requiring additional effort. My strong inclination would always be to see the world primarily through the images of the language of my birth. On the other hand, were I "naturally bilingual"—born into a bilingual family and society, schooled in the images of both from my earliest days—the inclusiveness of languages would not feel like a burden. It would feel natural.

My illustration admittedly suffers, because languages are thoroughly social inventions and learnings. Our bodies are not. While they have many social, learned meanings attached to them, they also have a biological givenness. My point, however, is this: We have been given "bilingual bodies." Even if one language has been developed more than the other, the second language is not foreign to us. It is not something we need to add on. It is just as originally part of us as the language with which, by accident of circumstances, we have become most familiar.

It is time to move beyond the usual meanings of androgyny. The vision for men is not to develop "feminine" energies (or for women to develop "masculine" energies). Rather, the vision for men is the fullest development of our *masculine* energies. But the issue is *fullness*. We are not talking only of phallic qualities. Penis is vulnerable, soft, receptive. Penis represents and invites the spirituality of the Via Negativa. But a penis is not "feminine"—it is as authentically masculine as is phallus. It bears qualities rooted in the fullness of the male's sexual experience, in the fullness of his body affirmation. So we who are men are simply invited to develop the masculine more richly. To speak this way is not to play word games. Linguistic sleight-of-hand tricks are abstractions. Incarnational reflection does not thrive on abstractions, but tries to represent bodily realities honestly.

Finally, it is important to recognize that each dimension of the male genital experience involves the other. Each of us experiences only one body, though in our experience there is the conjunction of apparent opposites. Paradoxically, the opposites are only apparently so. Each is implied by and contained within the other. Penis is always potentially phallus. The soft receptivity of penis implies relationality. But phallus is aroused as the genital aspects of relationship are anticipated or fantasized. So, also, the hard energy of phallus literally bears the signs of gentleness. The lover is amazed at the velvety texture and softness of the head of the man's rock-hard erection. Men know the vulnerability of their testicles and shield them from harm even during arousal and lovemaking. Indeed, male vulnerability is most present exactly at the spot where colloquial language locates male courage: "He has balls."[26]

Such is the marvelous conjunction of apparent opposites in the male's sexual body, a wholeness inviting him to richness of personhood. It is at the same time the bodily experienced invitation to richness of spirituality through the apparent opposites of Via Positiva and Via Negativa. Such is the golden ball of legend, representing connectedness and radiant energy.

Power and Size

One of the central issues in spirituality is *power.* [27] It is evident whenever personal beings are present to each other. Men's lives—and the lives of all those affected by patriarchy—have been dominated by one particular perception of power. It is *unilateral* power. It is also called zero-sum power, or the power of a closed energy system, inasmuch as it carries with it the assumption that there is only a limited quantity of power available, so that the more one person gets the less is available to the other. Unilateral power is nonmutual and nonrelational. Its purpose is to produce the largest possible effect on another, while being least affected by the other. Its ideal is control.

"In this view," writes Bernard Loomer, "our size or stature is measured by the strength of our unilateral power. Our sense of self-value is correlative to our place on the scale of inequality."[28] But the sense of self one has in this understanding is nonrelational, self-contained. It is the traditional masculine ideal of the Lone Ranger. The aim is to move toward maximum self-sufficiency. Dependency on others is weakness. But this kind of power, in reducing mutuality, produces estrangement among people. We are deadened to our interdependence and to the mystery of each other. This is unmodified phallic power.

Christianity has often embraced this view of power in its views of God. At such times it has seen God as omniscient, omnipotent, and controlling the world by divine fiat. This theology was built upon the same sexual dualism that split spirit from body. Spirit was seen as eternal, complete, and changeless, while body was temporal, incomplete, and changeable. God had unilateral power. "He" was perfect in his completeness and unaffected by those "below."

At the same time Christian theology embraced this unilateral understanding of power as applied to God, it had problems. The gospel message was quite clear that among people this was "worldly" power. Because such power was one-way and controlling, it seemed to be the antithesis of love. When Jesus renounced the power of the world, it was this kind of power he forsook. Thus, in Christianity a view of love as similarly one-way arose. It was the traditional interpretation of agape—a one-way divine love, a concern for the other with no concern for oneself. It was this kind of love that Christians were told to emulate. A one-sided love became the compensation for a one-sided power. One extreme was designed to offset a contrary extreme. The loss of eros and the goodness of the erotic, the confusion of selfishness with self-love—such were the prices exacted by unilateral power and unilateral love.

There is, however, another understanding of power. "This is the ability both to produce and to undergo an effect. It is the capacity both to influence others and to be influenced by others."[29] This is *relational* power. It is generative power, the power of an open energy system. Instead of a fixed, limited amount, the assumption is that shared power can generate more power. People are enhanced by this kind of power, mystery is affirmed, interdependence is celebrated. This, however, is not the power represented by the penis, but by the whole of the genitals and the whole of the body.

These distinctions concerning power bear on the problem of androgyny. Traditional androgyny begins with a combinationist assumption. It takes a fixed notion of the masculine (the active agent), a fixed notion of the feminine (the receiving, nurturing one) and tries to combine them in one person. However, in regard to power, both understandings of gender roles are deficient. The "feminine" principle has been under attack because it suggests a neurotic dependence on others and lack of sufficient autonomy. The "masculine" has been under attack because it suggests the urge to dominate others without being at the same time influenced by them. The point is that both are faulty. Adding one to another to achieve a balance is not the solution. Rather, the solution is understanding that both are definitions marred by fear and insecurity. The "feminine" fears self-dependence, while the "masculine" fears interdependence. Such fear is born of insecurity. It is the absence of authentic power.

Just as wholeness for either a man or a woman is not some combination of the masculine and the feminine, so also authentic relational power is not a neat combination of the active and the receptive. Relational power understands that the capacity to absorb the influence of another without losing the self's own center is as truly a quality of power as is the strength of exerting influence on another.

Loomer calls this kind of strength "size," the capacity to become large enough to make room for another within the self without losing the self's own integrity or freedom. "The world of the individual who can be influenced by another without losing his or her identity or freedom is larger than the world of the individual who fears being influenced. . . . The stature of the individual who can let another exist in his or her own creative freedom is larger than the size of the individual who insists that others must conform to his own purposes and understandings."[30]

Sexual experience always involves power. The experience of phallus without penis is unilateral power. The colloquial male ideal of the phallus is "two feet long, made of steel, and lasts all night." Phallus can handle multiple orgasms (or partners) without being reduced to flaccidity. The phallic perception of woman is as the receptacle for phallic power and emission. The ideal: affect without being affected.

In contrast, the man who affirms his whole sexuality knows that both phallus and penis are one. They are different but interdependent qualities of one male reality. Each at the same time is the other. In spite of the myth of phallic unaffectedness, men know that they are not made of steel, nor do they last all night. Phallus not only delivers effect but is also very much affected. In intercourse it is changed, transformed into penis. "Transformed" is a good word. Sometimes we use the language of death and resurrection about the male genital experience, but it is time to reassess that imagery. It can be highly misleading, even destructive. Yet I fear that the image is fairly common in the male psyche. It suggests that phallus is alive and then, when spent, dies. Penis, then, is the death from which phallus is raised once again. But this interpretation implies a very unilateral understanding of power. Only the phallus has power, the penis does not. Further, the suggestion is that, at least in the heterosexual experience, the woman is somehow associated with the "reducing" the phallus to flaccidity. Thus once again we make, even if unconsciously, the connection between woman and passivity. Now the woman somehow is responsible for the man's passivity, his loss of power and agency. But with the language of death and resurrection the psychic connections become more vicious. Now the phallus dies, and the connection is established between the woman and death. And death is assumed to be the enemy.

But when the phallus becomes penis it does not die. There is simply a change to another form of its life. When the phallus becomes penis it does not lose its power, except when that power is understood unilaterally. Rather, the penis has a different kind of power. It is now the man's genital sexuality expressing its capacity to absorb change. What was once hard and imperious is now soft and gentle. In both dimensions the man is experiencing his masculine power, and both are aspects of relational power. True power is mutuality, making claims and absorbing influence. It is different from the "mutuality" of external relatedness, which trades in force, compromise, and accommodation. It understands the paradox that the greatest influence often consists in being influenced, in enabling another to make the largest impact on oneself.

When a man so understands his sexuality he better understands true power, and when he understands power he better understands his sexuality. The same is true of size, for size and power are intimately related. However, "the wisdom of the world" about male genital size measures quality precisely in terms of quantity. Bigger is better. The masculinist fantasy says not only "made of steel" but also "two feet long." It does not matter that sexologists and sexual therapists tell us that the actual size of the male organ is quite irrelevant to effective sexual functioning and the quality of lovemaking—irrelevant except for one thing: too large an organ causes problems. Still, myth and fantasy persist. Pubescent boys still measure themselves and each other. The record holders are honored in the neighborhood gang. And, as noted earlier, Freud continues to be debunked in his contention that penis envy is a persistent phenomenon of the woman's unconscious; rather, it persists in the surreptitious, glancing comparisons made in the men's locker room.

In contrast to such worldly wisdom about size as quantitative, consider Loomer's description:

> By *size* I mean the stature of a person's soul, the range and depth of his [or her] love, his [or her] capacity for relationships. I mean the volume of life you can take into your being and still maintain your integrity and individuality, the intensity and variety of outlook you can entertain in the unity of your being without feeling defensive or insecure. I mean the strength of your spirit to encourage others to become freer in the development of their diversity and uniqueness. I mean the power to sustain more complex and enriching tensions. I mean the magnanimity of concern to provide conditions that enable others to increase in stature.[31]

When a man understands this meaning of size, his genital sexuality is less anxiously, more graciously celebrated. And when that is true, he also better understands the true meaning of size as criterion of genuine power.

If the themes of death and resurrection can be misleading when applied to penis and phallus, surely they have valid and profound meanings for our sexual and bodily lives more generally. The resurrection of the body in our experience means that mind and body no longer make war on each other, each trying to control or dominate the other. Now I can feel that I *am* my body, and that does not in any way contradict the fact that I am my mind or spirit. Death separates. Resurrection and life reunite. To be raised to life is to discover that I am one person. Body and mind are no longer felt to be distinct.

We usually have such an experience now and then. Most likely it is temporary, soon forgotten, for we have lived much of our lives with dualistic self-understandings and dualistic perceptions of reality at large. So body and mind fall apart again, each competing with the other for the prize of being me. Death sets in once more. But resurrections occur, and in those moments I know myself to be one. When that happens, the experience of oneness with myself brings with it the strong sense of connectedness with the rest of the world. I feel connected to—more than separated from—the people, creatures, and things among whom I live. They have their own identities, yet they also become part of me and I of them. My resurrection is the world's resurrection as I know that world.[32] The same applies to a man's genital perception. Resurrection occurs when penis and phallus are one, neither competing for the honor of being the man. When that happens there is true power—and authentic size.

Jesus as Sexual Man and Man of Power

Jesus as the Christ has been desexualized by most Christian piety throughout the ages. Sexual dualism has kept its sturdy grip, and incarnation, the real presence of God in human flesh, has been a scandal too great for most of the church to believe. A spiritualized God, acting in proper taste, simply would not do that sort of thing. Docetism, the belief that, in Jesus, God was not really humanly enfleshed but only appeared to be, was early declared a heresy by the church, but it still is very much alive. And about the most effective way of denying Jesus' full humanity has been to deny (outright or by embarrassed silence) his sexuality. Some of the early Christian Gnostics (who abhorred the flesh) represent the extreme. They could not even bring themselves to believe that Jesus needed to eat; he took food with his followers from time to time so not to alarm them. The thought of Jesus engaged in digestion, defecation, and urination would have appalled them. To the present-day Gnostics of whatever stripe, of course, the thought of Jesus' sexual arousal, erection, and orgasm is at best exceedingly poor taste and at worst blasphemous.

Just as popular piety has been aghast at the thought, theologians for the most part have simply avoided the issue of Jesus' sexuality other than to affirm his celibacy. Only rarely have they faced the question directly. William Phipps, one of the rare ones, has come to the conclusion that Jesus was probably married at one time.[33] Phipps finds no biblical evidence for Jesus' virginity, but rather finds a picture of Jesus as fully immersed in a sexuality-affirming Jewish culture, a culture which in fact rejected celibacy in both theory and practice. Jesus, who was hardly pictured as an ascetic by the Gospels, probably married sometime during those years about which we have no information (between ages twelve and thirty). Before his public ministry began, something—we do not know what—happened to his wife. The idea of a celibate savior, Phipps concludes, is not the product of the apostolic age but rather grew out of Christianity's later contact with the dualism of Hellenistic Greece.

I believe the case for Jesus' marriage is highly debatable. Had it happened, surely there would have been some apostolic mention of it. But whether or not Jesus married is not really the crux of the issue. His sexuality is, and investigations like that of Phipps help us to take the issue with greater seriousness. The question is not an esoteric one. If we who call ourselves Christian are unsure of the full humanity of him whom we call Truly Human, we shall be unsure of what full humanity means for us. If our image of authentic personhood in Jesus denigrates sexuality, we will do the same within ourselves.

Actually, some of the "secular theologians" have most effectively pressed the question of Jesus' sexuality. Nikos Kazantzakis and D. H. Lawrence have done so in literature. A particularly interesting inquiry is provided by a distinguished art historian, Leo Steinberg, in *The Sexuality of Christ in Renaissance Art and in Modern Oblivion.* [34] Steinberg observes that for a millennium of Christian history Jesus' sexuality was disregarded by theology and art, which focused virtually all attention on his divinity. Then came the Renaissance and the rediscovery of the glories of humanity.

Now devout Christian painters from Flanders to Florence removed the drapery from the figure of Jesus and purposely exposed his genitals. "In many hundreds of pious religious works, from before 1400 to past the mid-16th century, the ostensive unveiling of the Child's sex, or the touching, protecting or presentation of it, is the main action. . . . And the emphasis recurs in images of the dead Christ, or of the mystical Man of Sorrows. . . . All of which has been tactfully overlooked for half a millennium." [35] In the great cathedrals hung paintings of the Holy Family in which Mary herself deliberately spreads the infant's thighs so that the pious might gaze at his genitals in wonder. In other paintings the Magi are depicted gazing intently at Jesus' uncovered loins as if expecting revelation. In still others Jesus' genitals are being touched and fondled by his mother, by St. Anne, and by himself. So also in the paintings of the passion and crucifixion, the adult Jesus is depicted as thoroughly sexual. In some, his hand cups his genitals in death. In others the loincloth of the suffering Christ is protruding with an unmistakable erection.

Steinberg gives several interpretations of this Renaissance art. For one thing, it proved to the believer that Jesus' chastity was real and valid. Sexual abstinence without potency is an empty lesson. Abstinence is meaningful only if it is in combination with a vigorous sexuality. "Virginity, after all, constitutes a victory over concupiscence only where susceptibility to its power is at least possible." [36] Further, the shamelessness of exposing the infant Jesus' genitals for the admiration of others points back to our original innocence and points forward to our redemption from sin and shame, as the incarnation promises. His open adult sexuality depicted in the passion art promises our redemption. "Delivered from sin and shame, the freedom of Christ's sexual member bespeaks that aboriginal innocence which in Adam was lost. We may say that Michelangelo's naked Christs—on the cross, dead, or risen—are, like the naked Christ Child, not shameful, but literally and profoundly 'shame-less.' "[37] And, most fundamentally, the focus on the bodily sexuality of Jesus demonstrated the thoroughness, the completeness of the incarnation, God's choice to embody divinity in humanity. "Therefore, to profess that God once embodied [God]self in a human nature is to confess that the eternal, there and then, became mortal and sexual. Thus understood, the evidence of Christ's sexual member serves as the pledge of God's humanation."[38]

We have long known how deeply the Renaissance was committed to the goodness and beauty of the human body. Now we know how radically incarnational its theology was, at least as depicted through the world of art. A half millennium has elapsed since those Renaissance artists made their bold statements about the Christ's sexuality, and most people have chosen not to notice the obvious in their art Such is the "modern oblivion" about the issue. We continue in that oblivion to our profound deprivation.

Nevertheless, the affirmation of Jesus' sexuality raises difficult problems of another sort, precisely because he was male. The maleness of that one believed to be Christ has been used in countless ways as an instrument of patriarchal oppression. It has been used to "prove" the maleness of God, to outlaw women from ministry, to keep men in control. I agree fully with the protest against this oppressive theological misuse of Jesus' maleness, and I stand with those feminist women and men who despair over the church's tortured slowness in being redeemed on this matter. The central issue at stake is not Jesus' maleness but his *humanity,* to which his full human sexuality is crucial testimony. Indeed, Jesus' life, teachings, and the circumstances of his death all were remarkable protests against patriarchy.[39]

My concern at this point, however, is a different one: How can Jesus help men deal creatively with their own male sexuality? I believe that the ways are manifold, and what I have tried to suggest in this chapter are only a few of them. He stands as teacher, embodiment, and releaser of relational power—a judgment on our phallic unilateral power, but also an invitation to a full-bodied life-giving mutuality. His sexuality was present in his power, and his power was present in his healing sexuality.

Jesus stands as central symbol of the sexuality-spirituality dialectic. Renaissance artists saw in him the full and unified genitality of both phallus and penis, and portrayed him (to repeat Steinberg's words) "profoundly shame-less." Correspondingly, he strikingly embodied and taught the spirituality of both the Via Positiva and the Via Negativa, as is evident from the gospel accounts. He stands for us as symbol of our sexual-spiritual hope and possibility.

For human beings Jesus stands as clue to our authentic humanity in ways that far transcend the categories of sex and gender. In a less patriarchal age and culture than his, the person recognized as the paradigmatic Christ figure might well have been female. Yet Jesus was a first-century Jew, and he was male. This does not mean that through him maleness was certified as normative humanity. It does mean, however, that we who also happen to be male can find clues in him toward a richer and more authentic masculinity for ourselves. As a male I see this in the symbolism of Jesus' genital sexuality and the phallus-penis dialectic portrayed by Renaissance artists. I see in Jesus a compelling picture of male sexual wholeness, of creative masculinity, and of the redemption of manhood from both oppressiveness and superficiality. Yet countless women who are Christian also find in Jesus the intimate connection between their own female sexuality and spirituality. I suspect this is the case because Jesus embodies a sexual-spiritual reality that moves beyond our current understandings of androgyny.

I have argued that the notion of androgyny typically operates with a "combinationist" assumption. It begins with a fixed notion of masculine traits and a fixed notion of feminine traits. Then it moves to the contention that these fundamentally different qualities can and should be combined in any one individual regardless of biological sex. We have seen several problems with this concept. One of the major ones is the claim that we are called upon to develop a side of our personalities different from the one that seems rooted in our own particular bodies. The combinationist problem (in whatever form it occurs) is always grounded in an underlying dualism. Regarding androgyny, the dualism lies in the belief that the two sets of gender qualities are *essentially* different from each other, the assumption that authentic masculinity and authentic femininity are mutual opposites. From this assumption it follows that, in developing "the feminine" in himself, a man will add a different "something" on to that which is essentially himself. For example, he must acquire vulnerability and receptivity, qualities supposedly not natural to one with a male organ, to one equipped biologically to penetrate rather than to receive. I have suggested that men have encouraged this gender dualism through a one-sided definition of the masculine, a definition that magnifies the meanings of the phallus and neglects the reality of the penis.

Now the connection to be named is that between Christology and these gender issues. Like our struggle in recent decades to under-

stand gender issues through the concept of androgyny, the Christological concepts that have dominated the centuries of Christian
thought and piety have also been combinationist and dualistic. They
have largely maintained that divinity and humanity are two essentially opposite realities somehow brought into perfect combination
in one unique person. And when that occurred in Jesus it was a
miracle which happened once, was sufficient for all time, and was not
to be repeated.

But at least two major problems resulted from these prevailing
Christologies. First, divinity dominated humanity to the point that
Jesus' humanity became an illusion. Countless Christians believed
that Jesus Christ was actually God disguised as a human being. It
was the Superman / Clark Kent image. Jesus was the celestial visitor
from outer space who lived for a time on earth disguised as one of
us, did feats of superhuman power, and then returned to his glorious
home in the skies.[40] The second problem stemmed from the first. The
ordinary believer found it difficult to understand and internalize such
a meaning. Since this Christ event was defined by the church as
unique, by definition it was also out of the range of daily human
experience. It was utterly removed from the humanity people knew
to be their own. Hence, the Christic miracle became a formula, to
be accepted by faith and mediated by churchly sacraments for the
believer's salvation.

Both of these Christological problems have significant connections
to the gender issues before us. The divinity that seemed to dominate
and squeeze out Jesus' humanity was largely a phallic definition of
the divine. It was an understanding of God's power that was heavily
unilateral and one-directional. It was a zero-sum perception that
magnified divine power at the expense of human power. Suspicious
of the relational mutuality of a human Jesus and a divine God,
tradition perceived both power and love as one-way streets. So also
the masculine side of the androgyny formula has been equally phallic
and one-sided. Just as divine and human were seen as opposites,
likewise the masculine qualities and the feminine.

The Christological formula became abstract and confusing because it was removed from ordinary human experience. The same
has been true with the androgyny formula. When a man is called to
develop "his feminine side" but at the same time has been taught that
this feminine side is foreign to his own male bodily experience—
defined as phallus—a man finds himself striving to develop qualities
that seem strange to his own biological sexuality. Some sort of miracle seems necessary if the two opposites are to be combined.

But what if the realities—both Christological and sexual—are
significantly different from these accepted formulas? What if the

connections are essentially more intimate than we have supposed? How might that look?

I believe that Jesus did not understand himself to be ontologically different from other human beings. Nor did he intend to monopolize the Christic reality (the intimate communion of divine and human). His self-understanding and his mission were precisely the opposite. He did not aim to control and hoard the Christic possibility, but rather to release and share it among and with everyone. His uniqueness lay not in having two natures, one divine and one human, miraculously combined. Rather, he possessed the same human nature we all have, but remarkably and fully open in mutuality with God's loving power. We might recall that even John's Gospel, which contains an exalted view of Jesus as the Christ, maintains that all who believe in him (all who are open to his message of the presence of God) are given the power to become the sons and daughters of God.[41] The authentically human and the presence of the truly divine are, indeed, closer than we had imagined. When we embrace God we embrace that which is not foreign to our own human essence but that which makes us more truly human.

The same principle holds for our sexuality. Women are tracing for themselves the meanings of the richly conjunctive sexual-spiritual reality in Christ. No man can do that for women, nor should he try. We who are male have plenty to do for ourselves in this regard. But now the connections seem to be clearer than before.

Jesus remains the paradigmatic Christ-bearer of Christian faith and life. He embodied the divine-human communion with a fullness that awes, compels, judges, challenges, comforts, and attracts us. He is also the Christ-*barer,* the one who lays bare and open that Christic possibility for us all.

And now it seems clearer that this Christic possibility is intimately connected with our sexual wholeness. What is it to be a man? To be fully masculine is one of the two ways given to humanity of being fully human. To be fully masculine does not mean embracing something of gender foreignness, strange to our own male bodily experience. Rather, it means embracing the fullness of the revelation that comes through our male bodies. There is good phallic energy in us which we can claim and celebrate. It is the earthy phallus: deep, moist, and sensuous, primitive and powerful. The phallic energy in us is also solar: penetrating, thrusting, achieving, and with the desire for self-transcendence. Equally important *and equally male,* there is good penile energy in us. It is soft, vulnerable, and receptive. It is a peaceful power. It knows that size is not merely quantitative; more truly, it is that strength of mutuality which can be enriched by other life without losing its own center.

The orgasmic sexual experience brings its own revelation. The hard and explosive phallic achievement becomes in an instant the soft, vulnerable tears of the penis. Both are fully male. Both are deeply grounded in a man's bodily reality. Both dimensions of life are fully present when a man is most human. And to be fully human is to know the Christ—not as supernatural invader but as that reality truest to our own natures, and as that reality which intimately connects us with everyone and everything else.

SIX

New Ways
in Our Sexual Spirituality

It is frequently said that beginning in the 1960s a sexual revolution happened in our society. Indeed, there are some persuasive signs of just that. Significant changes occurred in numerous cultural and religious understandings about sex-role equality, about sex outside of marriage, about homosexuality, about single-parent families, about the more open portrayal and discussion of sexual matters, and so on. The shifts were spurred by a new American affluence, by the Pill, by the flood of women into the work force, by the Vietnam period's destabilization of traditional values, and by a new cultural emphasis on self-fulfillment. If none of these changes was total or without considerable resistance, still it is evident that something of major importance happened.

And, in the Orwellian year 1984, no less an authority than a *Time* cover story declared, "The revolution is over."[1] Veterans of the revolution, said *Time,* are both bored and wounded. The one-night stand has lost its sheen. "Commitment" and "intimacy" are in (helped by the scourges of herpes and AIDS). Celibacy is again a respectable option. The "me generation" is beginning to give way to the "we generation." Religious and political reaction to feminism, gay/lesbian rights, and the plurality of family forms has set in. If some changes seem lasting, there has been a decided movement back to more traditional sexual values. So said *Time*'s analysis, and it bears considerable truth.

Insofar as the "sexual revolution" involved sex for recreation it seemed promising to many, especially when it involved caring and tenderness. But it also led many people to a frantic search for sensation, thence to the deadening of sensation, and to erotic depersonalization. It is doubtful that most persons in our society want a return to the ways of sexual repression and discrimination. But what is increasingly clear is that they want something the revolution too frequently did not provide: to know the meanings of love. In that sense, the revolution is not over. It is just beginning. If the changes of the past quarter century did not usher in the wedding of sexuality and spirituality, hunger for that union was aroused, at the very least.

Some years ago, Paul Ricoeur observed that there were three major stages in western understandings of sexuality in relation to religion.[2] The earliest stage closely identified the two realms, with sexuality intimately incorporated into religious myth and ritual. The second stage, coming with the rise of the great world religions, brought separation. The sacred became increasingly transcendent and separate, while sexuality was demythologized and confined to a small part of the earthly order (procreation within institutionalized marriage). Sexuality's power was feared, restrained, and disciplined.

Ricoeur noted, however, that a third period now seems to be emerging, marked by the desire to unite sexuality once more with the experience of the sacred, a period prompted by more holistic understandings of the person and of the ways in which sexuality is present in all of human experience. If (with the second period) sexual expression is still seen as needing ordering and discipline, there is (with the first period) a renewed sense of its spiritual power.

I, too, believe that we are edging into that third period—very unevenly, yet truly. If that is accurate, the sexual revolution of the 1960s and 1970s was itself a very uneven experience. There were significant gains in releasing the constructive power of sexuality and in the call for sexual justice and equality. There were losses in the trivialization and mechanization of much sexual experience. Nevertheless, there has been an important opening to the third period.

Perhaps never before in the history of the church has there been so much open ferment about sexuality issues. The outpouring of treatises, debates, studies, and pronouncements, the formation of caucuses and movements bent upon reformation of religious-sexual attitudes or upon protecting them from unwanted change—all this has appeared to an unprecedented degree. In these developments there are signs that a paradigmatic shift in religious perceptions of human sexuality is under way. There are a number of signs of this shift that I find striking and have discussed elsewhere.[3] What I now realize, however, is that this shift of consciousness is of particular significance to *men*.

We who are men have been more firmly locked into the older paradigm than have women. We have had more social power, and as a result we have had greater ability to control the social definitions of sexuality. Those definitions in an earlier time seemed good and true—to many women as well as to men. Those definitions also served certain interests of men, often unrecognized by them. But those perceptions are rightly being questioned today, and radically so. In one sense, it would appear that men have most to lose from a significant shift in sexual perceptions—power and control. But that "loss" means greater justice for all. Moreover, men have an enormous amount to gain from these shifts—gains in the reunion of our sexuality and our spirituality, gains in our fuller humanity. In one way or another, I have alluded to each of these shifts in previous chapters. Now it is time to bring them together.

1. *There is a shift from "theologies of sexuality" to "sexual theologies."* Before the past two decades, the vast preponderance of Christian writers on sexuality assumed that the question before them was simply this: What does Christianity (the Bible, the tradition, ecclesiastical authority) say about sexuality? It was a one-directional question, moving from religious faith to sexual experience. Now we are also asking: What does our experience of human sexuality say about our perceptions of faith—our experience of God, our interpretations of scripture and tradition, our ways of living out the gospel?

The groundwork for this shift was laid many years ago. One of the hallmarks of the new theological liberalism in the nineteenth century was its insistence that human experience provides vital theological data. The liberals taught us that theological formulations are not static, unchanging truths revealed from on high. Rather, they are very human attempts to capture in word and thought our human experiences of God. In recent decades, several forms of liberation theology have embraced this insight in a new way. Third world and black Christians began to see that their own distinctive experiences of oppression and their possibilities of liberation afforded crucial insights into the nature of God's activity in the world.

Regarding sexuality, the important shift came from the feminist and lesbian/gay movements. Theirs was the claim that God is experienced in the movement toward liberation from sexual oppression. We must, they told us, move from experience to fresh understandings of the gospel as well as the other way around. Men are beginning to feel that hunger for liberation too. It has been slower in coming to consciousness, but it is emerging. It has varied names: hunger for friends, for living without the constant performance demand, for intimacy with lovers, for knowing one's own feelings, for knowing one's children, for the ability to play without having to win, for the possibility of living without premature death, for release from the violence men have inflicted upon the planet, for simply feeling good once again about being men. The names of the hungers are legion—these are only a few. Because men have been more split in their spirituality and their sexuality than have women, they have more healing from which to gain. There is a growing sense that theology must be grounded in this kind of experiential stuff. If we do not know the gospel in our bodies, perhaps we do not know it.

But there is more. There is the growing realization that one important reason why there has been too little sexual healing in the hearing of the gospel is that, under the male dominance of our theological tradition, many of our alienations have been written into our very understandings of the gospel. Some careful reexamination of the sexual-experiential lenses through which we have been perceiving the faith is needed.

The term "sexual theology," like the term "liberation theology," suggests this dialogical, two-directional inquiry. The two-way conversation model reminds us that theology cannot presume to look down upon human sexuality from some unaffected Olympian vantage point. It reminds us that every theological perception contains some elements and perceptions conditioned by sexual experience, and every sexual experience is perceived and interpreted through religious lenses of some kind. The consciousness of the difference between a unidirectional and a dialogical method is the difference between a theology of sexuality and a sexual theology.

2. *A shift is occurring, from understanding sexuality as either incidental to or detrimental to the experience of God, to understanding sexuality as intrinsic to the divine-human experience.* Sexual dualism, as we have seen, has marked much of the Christian tradition. Implicit in this dualism has been an assumption of divine impassivity, literally the *apathy* of God. If the body is marked by passion and if spirit is passionless, then bodily eros has no connection with the divine. God is without hunger, and the human hungers (of which sexuality, with its drive to connection and intimacy, is one of the most basic) seem to have no relation to our experience of God.

While the recent sexual revolution often seemed more intent upon self-fulfillment through unfettered pleasure than upon the quest for intimacy, it did prompt new theological reflection on the spiritual significance of sexual desire. If some of our Protestant forebears of three centuries ago were right in believing that companionship, not procreation, is God's central design for sexuality, then the human hunger for physical and emotional intimacy is of enormous spiritual significance. It ought not be denigrated as unbecoming to the spiritual life. Thus, theology has been giving new attention to the insight that, at its core, our sexuality is part of God's design that creatures not dwell in isolation and loneliness but in communion and community.

The integration of our sexuality into our practices of prayer and meditation is an important case in point. We are heirs of a male-dominated spirituality tradition that has deeply marked us by its dualisms and sex-negativism. Hence, insofar as our sexuality enters into our prayer at all, our first inclinations may be toward prayers of confession: for release from enslaving sexual desires; of guilt for wanting sex too much and making it the substitute for other things; of temptation or infidelity. The positive valuing of our bodies and our sexual experience may be more difficult, especially for men: thanksgiving for the tastes, sounds, and smells that come through a sensuous body; gratitude for grace known in orgasm with the lover; grateful delight in our own self-pleasuring possibilities; prayerful worries over erections, potency, pregnancies, desirability—all grounded in a sense of sex's goodness.

What we might yet absorb is the richness of sexual metaphor and image in communication with God. Some of the giants of the devotional life, among them Teresa of Avila and John of the Cross, Dame Julian of Norwich and Thérèse of Lisieux, frequently used images of sexual embrace, nursing at the divine bosom, and marriage to the divine. Such images expand our sexual and spiritual awareness. Ann and Barry Ulanov say it well:

> As we pray more, we listen to and hear more sides to our sexuality. We discover that there is no one model of what a man or a woman should be in their sexual selves. There are many sides to sexual identity. . . . The images we project upon God give valuable clues to the parts of ourselves we are struggling to accept and have others accept. We find among these projections sexual images for God, while at the same time we are aware of the inadequacy of the simple sexual identification of God as one sex or another, or even as androgynous. . . . God has all being, not just more being. Enlarging our understanding of human resources—recognizing that our sexuality is both more subtle and varied, both more masculine and more feminine than we thought—enlarges our understanding of the source of those resources.[4]

Such sexual praying, then, enlarges both our experience of God and of ourselves. We find new gratitude for the erotic desires we have felt and for their divine source. We contemplate the desirable qualities and bodies of the human others who attract us, and also find fresh mystery and attraction in the divine otherness. We find relief in facing honestly our sexual anxieties and compulsions, and find gratitude for a sexuality that is more wonderful and less fearful than we had sometimes experienced. Whether sexually celibate or genitally active, we are all lovers. "All are tutored in their love by the sexuality that defines a center of their being. And thus all are brought to their prayers, and made more in their prayers, by their sexual desire."[5]

Sexual prayer is but one way we can reclaim a more incarnational theology. Incarnation means that the most decisive experience of God lies not in doctrine, creed, or ideas but in Word made flesh—and in Word still becoming flesh. In all of this there is a challenge to the ancient dualism that fundamentally opposed spirituality and sexuality. There is a fresh opening to the reality that sexuality is intrinsic to the experience of God. Nikos Kazantzakis puts it this way: "Within me even the most metaphysical problem takes on a warm physical body which smells of sea, soil, and human sweat. The Word, in order to touch me, must become warm flesh. Only then do I understand—when I can smell, see, and touch."[6]

3. *There is a shift from understanding sexual sin as a matter of wrong sexual acts to understanding sexual sin as alienation from our intended sexuality.* The Christian tradition has had a pronounced tendency to define sexual sin as specific acts. This approach gained momentum during the early Middle Ages, when penitential manuals were first written detailing specific sins and their proper penances. Greatest attention was given to sexual matters. Indeed, in our heritage, "sin" and "morality" have had a markedly sexual focus—a "morals charge" never means economic injustice, one can be sure. Sexual sins thus became physiologically definable and capable of neat categorization. They were those particular acts either prohibited by scriptural texts or seen to be contrary to natural law: acts done with the wrong person, in the wrong way, or for the wrong purpose.

In most other respects, adequate Christian theology has always known that sin is not fundamentally an act but rather the condition of alienation or estrangement out of which harmful acts may arise. However, it has taken a long time to acknowledge that sexual sin is fundamentally alienation from our divinely intended sexuality. To put it overly simply but I hope accurately, sexual sin lies not in being too sexual but in being not sexual enough—in the way God has intended us to be. Such alienation, indeed, usually leads to harmful acts, but the sin is rooted in the prior condition.

Sexual sin is the dualistic alienation by which the body becomes an object, either to be constrained out of fear (the Victorian approach) or to be treated as a pleasure machine (the *Playboy* philosophy). It is the dualistic alienation in which females are kept from claiming their assertiveness and males from claiming their vulnerability. It lies in the alienation that finds expression in sexual violence, in Rambo-like militarism, in racism, in ecological abuse.

The uncompleted sexual revolution began to see some of this. In its superficial and exploitive moments it simply wanted to wipe away the category of sexual sin. "If it feels good, do it." In its better moments, there were insights that sexual sin was something different from, and more than, particular acts that could be neatly defined.

Men typically experience sexual alienation in a variety of ways. We males are more alienated from our bodies than are most women. Our bodies seem instrumental to us, and their deep emotions are often strange and frightening. All too frequently, violence becomes a substitute for our tears. Sexual alienation includes the loneliness fed by the fires of sexual fears. Fear of intimacy with other males is fed by homophobia, while fear of intimacy with women is inhibited by sexist distancing and internalized performance-failure fears. We have looked at these and other forms of male sexual sin in earlier chapters.

One of the most evident forms of sexual alienation that so many males feel, however, is simply the lack of a secure and solid sense of manhood. In most so-called (and probably misnamed) "primitive" societies, the rites of passage from boyhood into manhood were clear. Though they often involved violent feats of courage and endurance of pain, they still bonded the adolescent male to the men of the tribe and gave him a clear sense that he was now a man. In the absence of such initiations, we attempt other rituals in order to fill the void. But they do not satisfy. The driver's license and feats of automotive daring, fraternity initiations, diplomas, drinking and drug rituals, scoring on the athletic field—none of these seems to bring a lasting sense that the boy has become a man. Perhaps our closest approach to the ancient manhood-confirming ritual is the military experience, which secludes younger men with older men who thrust upon them tests of psychological and physical endurance. In the absence of such initiation rites, many young men seek their rites of passage with the opposite sex. They ask young women for something that the culture has not given them—their manhood. "Certain of her femininity and of her pregnability, she dares to wait until the time is right. Insecure about his masculinity and obsessed with proving it—to himself and his buddies, if not to her—he needs to score in order to feel that he has made the team."[7] But his conquest is still private; done in the dark of night, the proof of his manly virility vanishes in the light of day, a rite of passage only in his own mind, unconfirmed by the larger society.

Sexual alienation—and its unending quest for masculine identity—is rooted for many males in the father-son experience. The search, for many men, is lifelong. Samuel Osherson observes, "The interviews I have had with men in their thirties and forties convince me that the psychological or physical absence of fathers from their families is one of the great underestimated tragedies of our times."[8] Boys become men carrying a "wounded father" within, their conflicted inner sense of masculinity rooted in their experience of their fathers as absent, rejecting, or incompetent. Perhaps nothing would be the same in our world—whether religion, politics, science, business, education, or art—if men spent more time in the world of the infants and toddlers they have sired.

My own childhood came during the Depression years, and like many of my generation I experienced my father as having a mysterious, remote quality. I knew little of his inner life, what he thought and felt as a man. He was a large, strong figure to me, one whom I could neither approach nor avoid. His expectations were high, and he held his sons to them. I felt his pride in my achievements, his judgment on my failures. Like many men, he showed his love more symbolically than through his words: working hard, providing well, being a responsible and respected community leader, occasionally showing a rough tenderness. His love was expressed from a distance. Even then, he could withdraw his love, and when it was withdrawn it sometimes felt as though he might never come back. One part of me wished desperately to be a good son, while another part deeply rebelled.

Other men report experiencing their fathers somewhat differently from the way I did. Some of these sons who grew up in the 1960s and 1970s felt the impact of both the women's movement and the Vietnam War. They were drawn to those women who expressed justice and caring, and abandoned the fathers who seemed to express masculine oppression. In any event, the search for the father is the quest for authentic masculine strength and goodness. The alienation from the father that many men feel throughout their lifetimes is one very important illustration of sexual sin.

These are some of the real issues of sexual sin. It is no small shift in consciousness to move from understanding sexual sin as essentially wrong or bad acts to the realization that alienation from our intended sexuality is the core problem. None of us escapes such woundedness, and men carry their own particular kinds.

4. *We are experiencing a shift from understanding salvation as anti-sexual to knowing that there is "sexual salvation."* Because spiritualistic dualism has so conditioned much of the Christian tradition, we have inherited a disembodied notion of salvation. Salvation somehow means release from the lower and fleshly life into the higher life of the spirit. Indeed, popular piety has typically viewed the saints as asexual, surely without sexual needs and desires, sometimes even without genitals.

In its better moments, the sexual revolution convinced many Christians that an incarnationalist faith embraces the redemption of our alienated sexuality as well as other estranged dimensions of our lives. Justification by grace signifies God's unconditional, unmerited, radical acceptance of the whole person. God, the Cosmic Lover, graciously embraces not just a person's disembodied spirit but the whole fleshly self—the meanings of which theology is only beginning to explore.

Sanctification, the second classical salvation term, means growth in holiness (or wholeness and health—the root word is the same). Unfortunately, much in our tradition has taught us that sanctification involves the denial of our sexuality or the escape from our bodies. We are beginning to realize, however, that increasing sexual wholeness is part of our redemption intended by God. Sexual sanctification can mean growth in bodily self-acceptance, in the capacity for sensuousness, in the capacity for play, in the diffusion of the erotic throughout the body rather than in its genitalization, and in the recovery of lost dimensions of our sexuality.

A crucial part of sexual salvation for many men lies in finding their fathers. In our church's nave are five beautiful stained-glass windows depicting Jesus' parables. During worship I find my eyes regularly drawn to one window more than to any of the others. It is the forgiving father embracing the prodigal son. While this parable as Jesus told it is immeasurably rich in meaning, its central point is quite clear: the utterly gracious, profoundly accepting, unbelievably forgiving love and presence of God freely offered to us without our earning or deserving. In the story the father doesn't even wait to hear the son's confession, so eager is he to run to meet him, embrace him, kiss him, welcome him home, and begin the reunion party. All of that is quite clear from the parable. Yet, in my Sunday morning musings I find myself yearning to have that window also signify the son embracing the prodigal father. I yearn for the two simply to find reunion.

At the end of Arthur Miller's *Death of a Salesman,* Biff, now a young man, is desperately searching for connection with his father. Taller than Willy, in tears Biff leans down and hugs him. But Willy sits there dispassionate, uncomprehending, shrugging his shoulders at his wife, on whom he depends to interpret his feelings. Unmoved, unmoving, he doesn't hug his son back. Several years ago I saw Dustin Hoffman playing Willy Loman. Before going to the play I had read *The New Yorker* review, in which the only complaint about this powerful production was that it was difficult to hear some of the lines toward the end because there were so many muffled sobs and so much nose-blowing in the audience. It was true the night I was there, and mine were among them. The play's end brings no healing between father and son. Willy dies and Biff appears destined to live out the wounds and the void. But it need not be that way.

Healing comes in different ways. My own process has been a slow one. As I have said, I was twenty-two and in the army when my father suddenly died. Good soldier that I was, I didn't cry. Nor did I deal with the terrible complexity of emotions that any death brings to those in the family. I buried all that in his grave with him. It was fully twenty-four years later that an intense group experience at the Esalen Institute opened up the grave to expose grief, anger, resentment, sadness, tears. Nor did months of these feelings now close to the surface end the process. In therapy several years after that, I realized how much unfinished business remained. I had to confront the unfulfilled longings for words of love, for physical tenderness, for intimate companionship. I had to uncover some painful memories of abuse and of fear of my father's power, and I had to deal with my rage. A turning point came one day when the therapist challenged me: "When will you be ready to forgive your father?"

Resurrection can begin when we who are men find ourselves willing to enter our fathers' worlds as best we can, feeling into what they might have experienced and felt with their own fathers and embracing their pain. It begins when we deal with our own uncomfortable feelings about our unmet needs to have been held by our fathers, when we deal with our own betrayals and unatoned sins toward our fathers. It begins when we let go of our harbored wishes for the perfect father who would have given us everything we needed to live our lives. This process can be harder when our fathers are dead or inaccessible to us, but the process is possible.

Reconciliation with the father may be possible, and that is what many men crave. But even when it is not, healing the wounded father within is possible, as Osherson says: "That is because the essential elements in healing are the internal image of the father and the sense of masculinity that the son carries in his heart. The son needs to be able to understand the always poignant reasons why the past was the way it was, thus freeing him from his sense of having been betrayed by the father or having been a betrayer of him. [The son] needs to explore satisfying ways to be male that reflect his own identity. We can recognize that we are our father's son without feeling that we have to accept and love everything about him or all that happened between us."[9]

In that stained-glass window, at times it is not clear to me which figure is the prodigal, son or father, when I think of both as human figures. I am convinced that sons must often forgive and graciously embrace their fathers. I know I need that from my own son. When the figures represent the divine and the human, is it any different? In Jesus' parable it was clearly one way, not the other. But in a curious sense, the question is not finally answered by that affirmation, as important as it is. Those who have struggled most profoundly with the problem of evil—as Elie Wiesel struggles with the Holocaust—have agonizingly and angrily posed the question of God's need for forgiveness. How else can one understand the plight of a twelve-year-old Sarah who became the sexual toy of the German officers in the prison camp? What kind of God can allow this to happen, a God who "tortures twelve-year-old children"? Do we live in an "immense brothel we call the universe," whose doorkeeper is God?[10]

While this is not the place, nor do I have the capacity, to struggle with that genuine question as it deserves, it is appropriate to raise it that we might be strangely reminded of one thing: our falsely masculinized and confused God images. Our patriarchal theological tradition has led us to confusion about "God the Father." Granted, Jesus' use of "Father" ("Abba") was radical in its transformation of the traditional notion of divine transcendence and distance. But our uses of the image have usually failed to capture Jesus' meanings. In practice, we create God in our own image—now in the image of the human father we have experienced—and then find "God" too often distant, absent, demanding, and conditional in "his" love. Such deity surely needs to be forgiven. Indeed, we are surprised when "he" can be so gracious to the prodigal son. One can say, of course, it is still we who need forgiveness, *metanoia,* a turning around in our impoverished projections upon the divine. And that is largely true. But in a curious way—known deeply only to the Wiesels and others who have looked unblinkingly into the inexplicable face of human suffering, but known fleetingly by most of us who have reflected at all upon pain—the awful transcendence of God must be forgiven if we are to be reunited with the gracious divine immanence.

What is divine and what is human get all mixed up in our experience, in our memories, in our emotions, even when we find it possible to make neat rational theological statements about it all. I must live with the recognition that some Sunday mornings as I look at that window, I am not sure who is the prodigal or where are the boundaries of divinity and humanity. What *is* clear to me is that there is a deep healing between them.

Surely there are rhythms in human father-son relationships in which now one and now the other is forgiver and forgiven, embracer and embraced. There is heroism and there is failure in our fathers' lives, and in ours. To identify with the good in our fathers, "to feel how we are like them, as well as the ways we are different from them . . . [brings] a fuller, trustworthy sense of masculinity . . . [and] the sure, quiet knowledge that men as well as women are lifegiving forces on earth."[11]

5. *We are seeing a shift from an act-centered sexual ethics to a relational sexual ethics.* The sexual revolution in this society coincided with some important shifts in Christian ethical thought. For all of its oversimplifications Joseph Fletcher's *Situation Ethics* in the mid-sixties aroused an extraordinary interest in ethical rethinking on the part of many people not otherwise inclined to the technicalities of professional ethics. The more sophisticated approaches to an ethics of response and contextual-relational ethics, differently expressed by such thinkers as H. Richard Niebuhr and Paul Lehmann, had a major impact on ethical thought in the same decade. In the years since that time, these ethical styles have had increasing influence in Christian thinking, including feminist ethics.

In contrast, act-oriented ethics has dominated much of the Christian tradition, particularly when applied to sexual matters. Such ethics assumed that the rightness or wrongness of a particular sexual expression could be determined by the objective moral nature of the act itself, a value intrinsic in that act, a meaning unchanged by the relational context or situation. Thus, ethicists and churchly authorities could catalog various sexual acts—masturbation, same-sex intercourse, heterosexual intercourse (premarital, marital, extramarital)—as objectively and intrinsically right or wrong. The alternative to such clarity seemed to be a normless subjectivism, particularly dangerous in sexuality issues, where passions run high.

It is significant that, over the centuries, the Christian insistence on this kind of ethical precision and control was particularly evident regarding sex. It was also present to a noticeable degree in family issues and in medical ethics. But in the spheres of human activity that seemed less "bodily" and "personal"—economics, politics, war and peace—Christian ethics showed more willingness to take the relativities of contexts into account. That pattern ought not surprise us. The ethical tradition has been dominated by men, and men have had less comfort with the sexual, the bodily, and the personal. Further, these are areas that a patriarchal worldview has identified with the feminine, hence they appear fraught with greater anxiety for men and more in need of being controlled.

Roman Catholic sexual ethics, with its strong natural-law tradition and clearly defined ecclesiastical teaching authority, has been somewhat more inclined toward objective sexual norms than has Protestant ethics, with its more scriptural orientation. Both, however, have been more objectivistic and act-focused in sexuality issues than in almost any other moral sphere. In recent years, however, many in both traditions have moved toward a new and creative sexual ethics. Act-oriented ethics has appeared inadequate, not only in cases with unique contexts and meanings but in light of a growing

recognition that Christian sexual ethics has been inadequately integrated into a holistic spirituality. If sexuality is the physiological and
psychological grounding of our capacities to love, if our destiny after
the image of the Cosmic Lover is to be lovers in the richest, fullest
sense of that good word, then how do our sexual ethics figure into
our spiritual destiny? What are our creative and fitting sexual responses to the divine loving? What are the appropriate sexual meanings to embody the meanings of Word becoming flesh?

These are the questions that seem increasingly appropriate to
many. For example, in a promising and controversial book published
in the late 1970s, a group of Roman Catholic scholars proposed that
Catholic sexual ethics stop centering upon procreation, natural law,
and the physical contours of sexual acts. The focus, they argued,
needs to be different. "Wholesome human sexuality is that which
fosters a *creative growth toward integration.* Destructive sexuality
results in personal frustration and interpersonal alienation."[12]
Growth and integration are promoted by self-liberating, other-en-
riching, honest, faithful, socially responsible, life-serving, and joyous
sexual expressions. These are marks of a gospel ethic of love.[13] In
more recent years, Rome's clear retreat from such Vatican II directions as this is evidence that the paradigm shift is still very uneven.
The tenacity with which Protestant fundamentalists hold to an act-
oriented, objectivist sexual ethics is similar evidence. Yet countless
Christians know that a significant ethical change is under way.

Such changes in ethical style—and the resistance to them—have
direct connections with issues of masculine spirituality. As one who
works in academic life (a theological seminary), I have been increasingly aware in recent years how abstract and hyperrationalized is
much of our theology and ethics. Imagination and feeling have been
underdeveloped in this male-dominated discursive tradition, and in
myself as a practitioner. As a typical young male I was conditioned
to protect myself against bodily attack and defend myself against the
perils of the vulnerable emotions. For many years I was largely out
of touch with a whole range of bodily feelings.

But such male alienation takes a terrible toll. It leads us into
abstracting ourselves from the bodily concreteness of others. To
stand in the ashes of that village in Vietnam and say, "We had to
destroy this village in order to save it," is abstractionism that lured
a man into an exaggerated, violent sense of reality.

When ethics loses its attention to flesh-and-blood concreteness,
then bloodless abstractions, principles, and concepts begin to take
on a life of their own. They become more real than people, animals,
plants, and earth. What is lost, however, is not only concreteness
but also the sense of connection—the deep, bodily sense of our

profound connectedness to everything else. The recovery of the body brings with it the realization that the fundamental reality of our lives is not our separation but our relatedness, a surprising revelation to the male conditioned to a Lone Ranger mentality. Yet, running through almost every page of the Bible is faith's perception of the deep relationality of life. The metaphors are connectional: covenant, the people of Israel, the body of Christ, the vine and the branches.

"Whoever does not receive the [realm] of God like a child shall not enter it" (Mark 10:15). And what is the little one's knowledge? As children we learned (until we were taught otherwise) that the fundamental reality with which we deal in life is not disconnected objects but relationships. As infants we were literally loved into our human being. We were given the human gifts of relating by being held and sensuously nurtured by the parental body. We were talked into our capacity for speech, communicated into our possibilities of communion. We learned the connectedness of life through our bodily space. We learned prepositions—in, over, under, between, beyond—and each one depended on an instinctive sense of our own bodily location in relation to the rest of the world.

To know myself as profoundly relational is to know myself as body. All our relationships are mediated through our bodies. In our emotions we interact with the world. In our sexual, sensuous selves our sense of relatedness is grounded. It is our sense of bodily integrity that grounds our power with others and our capacities for vulnerability with them. When I sense the holiness of my own body, I begin to sense the holiness of every other body.[14]

Ethics involves critical reflection on the moral life. Ethical reflection needs concepts such as principles and rules. These are the handles we get on experience in order to talk about morality with others. They make public discourse possible. But when we treat abstractions as though they were actual existing beings, we lose contact with the richness, the variety, the connectedness, and the ambiguities of life. We become too tidy about things that are not tidy. We use our ethics to control more than to liberate persons into life-giving relationships. It is true of all areas of our ethics, but our sexual ethics are a particularly telling example. These are things that women have known better than men. But we are learning them, and our ethics are changing in the process.

6. *A shift is happening, from understanding the church as asexual to understanding it as a sexual community.* Through most of its history, the church has viewed sexuality as either incidental or inimical to its life. But the sexual revolution resulted in a growing self-consciousness and empowerment of the sexually oppressed. Religious feminism articulated the ways in which the church has *always* been a sexual community—the ways it has incorporated patriarchy into its language, worship, theological imagery, leadership patterns, and ethics. A rising gay/lesbian consciousness performed a similar function in regard to the church's heterosexism. Gradually, other groups—singles (including the widowed and divorced), the aging, those with handicapping conditions, the ill—have begun to recognize how churchly assumptions and practices have sexually disenfranchised them. The church, indeed, has always been a sexual community, though in ways often unrecognized and oppressive.

Another impetus for claiming and reforming the church as a sexual community has come from the rising hunger to reunite sexuality and spirituality. The realization that Protestant worship has been marked by a masculinist focus on the spoken word and by a suspicion of bodily feelings has suggested the need to explore and touch the varied senses more inclusively. The fact that Christian education has seriously ignored sex education has prompted the attempt to address sexual meanings as a part of faith's journey, for young and old. The recognition that most theology has given only lip service to the incarnation, failing to take ongoing incarnationalism seriously in both method and content, has inspired an effort to explore the doing and meaning of body theology.

In one sense, we must do theology simply because we *are* body-selves. As such, we are impelled into a relational existence, and we need to ask what it is all about. Through our bodily eros we are drawn into intercourse—verbal, tactile, social, political, economic, sexual intercourse—with others. And, as beings who seek meaning, we need to ask about these occasions of human intercourse. What is their value? Are they life-denying or life-giving? Do they thwart or fulfill our deepest needs as persons and as communities? What is their ultimate meaning?

If we must do theology because we are body-selves drawn into all sorts of intercourse with other body-selves, we who are Christian also theologize in certain ways because we are part of the body of Christ. Because we are Christian we deal with the centrality of a Christic revelation of God. Traditional Christology, as we have seen, all too frequently has drawn our attention away from our own bodily life. In focusing upon the singular divinity of one person and portraying that divinity as overwhelming his humanity, something else was substituted for radical incarnation. What was substituted was the belief in an unchanging, unilateral transcendent power whose divine love was utterly different from human love, whose divine body was utterly different from our bodies. Suppressed was the compelling experience of incarnation as the meaning and reality, the healing and life-giving power of our embodied relationships with others.

Recovering the conviction that the Christic reality is the invitation for us all, we will recover Luther's insight about being "Christ to the neighbor"—and we will meet the Christ in the neighbor. It is not that we or our neighbors are the *source* of healing and empowerment. But when healing and empowering do occur we have been the necessary *meeting place* of God and human flesh, the crucial if fragmentary embodiment of God. Most likely it will be, again, in that surprising reversal portrayed in Jesus' parable: the embodied God in the one who is hungry, thirsty, strange, naked, sick, imprisoned in varied kinds of prisons. The embodied God in one who knows God's absence and thus paradoxically mediates the divine presence, the one who mediates God's weakness and vulnerability, thereby eliciting another's and for the moment bonding us together in life-giving communion.

Such Christic experience reshapes notions about the church's ministry. The ministry models so familiar to men, be they clergy or laity, are usually different. The familiar is more hierarchical, more unilateral in its understanding of power, more answer-giving, more a ministry exercised from a position of strength to those perceived to be in need. A space-making, question-asking, self-disclosing ministry of mutual vulnerability may feel strange, for it is not shaped by one-sided phallic understandings. But it is the sort of ministry that connects people and enhances their true size.[15] It is the sort of ministry through which Christ again and again takes form in community.

Indeed, one of the significant facts about the church's life in the past couple of decades has been its movement—often hesitant and fumbling, sometimes rancorous and divisive, occasionally creative and promising—to reclaim and re-form itself as a sexual community. Much of the recent ferment in theology and ethics, in worship and pastoral care, in leadership and education has been a result. When we forget that the church is a sexual community, we only allow unreflective, uncriticized, and often unjust expressions of our sexuality to shape its life. When we remember, however, we have fresh awareness of the transformative power and presence of the body of Christ.

7. *There is a shift from understanding sexuality as a private issue to understanding it as a personal and public issue.* Sexual issues will always be intensely personal, engaging some of the deepest feelings, desires, self-understandings, pleasures, and pains of each individual. However "personal" is different from "private." One mark of Victorian sexuality was its privatization. Not only was sexuality not to be talked about, it was to be confined to a small portion of one's private life. Indeed, sexuality was reduced to sex—"the privates." But this, quite literally, was idiocy. (The Greek word for *idiot* refers to the person who attempts to live the private life, ignorant of and unconcerned about the public domain.)

One of the church's recent discoveries is the public dimension of sexuality issues. On the social-action agenda of mainline denominations today are sexual-justice issues regarding gender and sexual orientation. No longer foreign to church concern are the issues of abortion, family planning and population control, sexual abuse and violence, pornography, prostitution, reproductive technologies, varied family forms, sexually transmitted diseases, teenage pregnancy, and the reassessment of men's lives. The list could go on. All these issues are obviously sexual, and all are public.

Even newer than this development is the nascent discovery of sexual dimensions in issues that previously had not appeared to have them. In chapter 4 we saw some of the sexual roots of social violence. To be sure, the sources and manifestations of violence are complex, and no single factor provides full explanation. But what do we make of the competitiveness, the cult of winning, the armoring of emotions, the tendency to dichotomize reality, the abstraction from bodily concreteness, the exaggerated fear of death that is manifested in morbid fascination with it? All of these feed social violence, and all are deeply related to sexual distortions, particularly a false masculinism.

Years ago, James Weldon Johnson observed that the sex factor is deeply rooted in the race problem as well, and rooted so deeply that it is often not recognized. Historically, white males' categorization of women ("either virgins or whores") proceeded along racial lines: white women were symbols of delicacy and purity, whereas black women symbolized an animality that could be sexually and economically exploited. White men projected their guilt onto the black male, fantasizing him as a dark supersexual beast who must be punished and from whom white women must be protected. Black mothers nurtured their sons to be docile, hoping to protect them from white male wrath. That upbringing in turn complicated black marriages and led to certain destructive attempts to recover black "manliness." We are the heirs of a distorted racial history in which sexual dynamics have been a major force.

Sexual dynamics are pervasive in our ecological abuse. We are heirs also of a powerful and hierarchical sexual dualism that has shaped much of our understanding of nature. The hierarchy begins with God on top of the chain of being, understanding God as "nonmaterial spirit," and continues downward to "nonspiritual matter" at the bottom, with the bottom believed to be inferior and of value only as it serves that which is above it. In between are men (more like God), followed by women, then children, animals, and plants. It is a clear chain of command.[16] Numerous dualistic dynamics then contribute to our alienation from the earth. Men, inclined to treat their bodies as machines, as possessions to be disciplined and used, treat the earth correspondingly. And the earth becomes feminine, "mother nature," the lower half of the dualism, alien from and subject to the male consciousness. Dominion of the earth becomes domination. Rape of the earth ensues. Our insatiable appetites for production and consumption poison the air, rain acid upon the lakes, destroy the topsoil, and allow the extinction of many species of life to pass unmourned.

We are just beginning to see more ecological consciousness in our society growing out of enlightened human self-interest. We are utterly dependent on the products of the earth's four basic biological systems—grasslands, croplands, forests, and fisheries—and the global per capita productivity of each of these four systems has now peaked and is declining.[17] We are beginning to realize that we are doing ourselves in by our destruction of the natural environment and that it is in our own best interests to reverse the trend. But a deeply transformed ecological consciousness cannot come through self-interest alone, however enlightened that may be. It must involve a new erotic sensibility, a sensibility that is rooted in a transformed male consciousness.

And what might that mean? Eros is the passion for connection, the enemy of dichotomy and disconnection. A new male consciousness will refuse to embrace the gulf between human beings and the remainder of the universe, an assumption so much part of our tradition. Scientists have encouraged that assumption by characterizing the rest of the universe as objective and mechanical. Humanists have contributed by their emphasis on the radical uniqueness of the human mind. A pervasive dualistic way of thinking has been the result. But the erotic sensibility sees continuity and connection as fundamentally more real and significant than discontinuity and disconnection. We human beings are continuous with nature.

Likewise, the disjunction between nature and history falls before the erotic sensibility. Nature is not just mechanical cause and effect. Nature itself is historical, with spirit indwelling in each form of life, spirit biomorphically appropriate to that life form. The universe itself is a great being that is born, grows, and presumably will die. The critical moments of change in its growth are not simply the result of blind mechanical necessity but the result of spirit and intelligence indwelling in life.

Our conversion to recognize and participate in spirit-filled nature calls for an erotic transformation of our ways of thinking White western male rationality has emphasized the linear and the dichotomous: reality is divided into dualisms of the higher and the lower, the good and the bad, one to dominate and the other to be controlled. Such thought patterns are encouraged by the dominance of left-brain functions and the suppression of right-brain capacities, patterns more typical of males. Such perceptual patterns are reinforced by every hierarchy of social oppression—white people over those of color, rich over poor, heterosexual over homosexual, and of course men over women. Linear thinking categorizes, dichotomizes, focuses on parts, and misses the patterns of relationality and interdependence. But we need a whole-brain consciousness, the connectedness of the whole person.

The ways we express ourselves sexually in the bedroom are connected with everything else. There is a difference between narrowly genital, orgasm-focused sex and making love. An erotic consciousness bears the promise of the sensuous body-self making love with the earth. The universe is a participatory universe. The Hebrew word *yada'*, "to know," also means "to make love sexually." It is mutual and participatory, neither dominant and submissive nor active and passive. It is full-bodied loving, not simply a conjunction of genitals where there is penetrator and penetrated. It is when two knowers and two knowns reveal their connectedness. Such loving is the stuff of a new ecological awareness.

Our theology and our spirituality have been tardy in grappling with sexuality's public connections, but it is coming. Two decades ago Teilhard de Chardin observed:

> The prevailing view has been that the body . . . is a *fragment* of the Universe, a piece completely detached from the rest and handed over to a spirit that informs it. In the future we shall have to say that the Body is the very Universality of things. . . . *My* matter is not a *part* of the Universe that I possess *totaliter:* it is the *totality* of the Universe possessed by me *partialiter.* [18]

The sexual revolution of the past quarter century is mostly over, and some of its superficial and exploitive forms of freedom have proved to be just that. Hurt, boredom, and disease have sobered more than a few—and the forces of religious and political reaction rejoice. Nevertheless, this revolution was a harbinger of a much more significant change, which Ricoeur foresaw. That change is just beginning. It is uneven, misunderstood, and resisted, as well as eagerly welcomed and hoped for.

This will not be the first time in Christian history that a major shift has taken place in the perception of sexuality. Recall that in the seventeenth century some Protestants began to affirm that loving companionship, not procreation, is the central meaning of sexuality. This religious revolution is still unfinished. But even more far-reaching changes are now taking place.

The changes in our perception and experience of male sexuality and masculine spirituality are an enormously important part of this more fundamental revolution. As we who are men increasingly become part of this process, we will become better lovers. We will become better friends of God, of our world, and of ourselves. We will know in a new way that the Word continues to become flesh and dwell among and within us. And as that happens, our male energy will be more life-giving than we have yet known.

W. H. Auden, in his Christmas oratorio "For the Time Being," has the magi explain their strange mission in these words:

> To discover how to be truthful now . . .
> To discover how to be living now . . .
> To discover how to be loving now . . .
> To discover how to be human now . . .[19]

They were wise men indeed.

Notes

CHAPTER ONE: Male Sexuality and Masculine Spirituality

1. See Deryck Calderwood, "Male Sexual Health," *SIECUS Report,* vol. 13, no. 2 (Nov. 1984), pp. 1–5. I am indebted to Calderwood for much of the information in the next several paragraphs.

2. See Kenneth Solomon, "Effect of Masculine Behavior on Life Expectancy," *Medical Aspects of Human Sexuality,* vol. 17, no. 10 (Oct. 1983), pp. 146–148.

3. Maurois's insight is described by Rollo May, *Love and Will* (New York: W. W. Norton & Co., 1969), p. 170.

4. Walter Williams, *The Spirit and the Flesh: Sexual Diversity in American Indian Culture* (Boston: Beacon Press, 1986). Cf. James A. Doyle, *The Male Experience* (Dubuque, Iowa: William C. Brown, Pubs., 1983), p. 83.

5. Studs Terkel, *Working* (New York: Pantheon Books, 1977), p. 55.

6. Jonathan Cobb and Richard Sennett, *The Hidden Injuries of Class* (New York: Random House, 1973), p. 156.

7. Michael S. Kimmel, "Teaching About Men," *Journal of the National Association for Women Deans, Administrators, and Counselors,* vol. 49, no. 4 (Summer 1986), p. 18.

8. Michael S. Kimmel, "Judaism, Masculinity, and Feminism," *Changing Men,* no. 18 (Summer/Fall 1987), p. 14.

9. For excellent theological reflections on some of these issues, see James E. Dittes, *When Work Goes Sour* (Philadelphia: Westminster Press, 1987); David J. Maitland, *Looking Both Ways: A Theology for Mid-Life* (Atlanta: John Knox Press, 1985) and *Aging: A Time for New Learning* (Atlanta: John Knox Press, 1987).

10. Elie Wiesel, *One Generation After* (New York: Random House, 1970), p. 173. See Robert McAfee Brown, *Elie Wiesel: Messenger to All Humanity* (Notre Dame, Ind.: University of Notre Dame Press, 1983), pp. 193–200.

11. See Kimmel, "Teaching About Men," pp. 14–15.

12. See Joseph H. Pleck, "The Male Sex Role: Definitions, Problems, and Sources of Change," *Journal of Social Issues,* vol. 32, no. 3 (1976), pp.

155–164; Pleck, *The Myth of Masculinity* (Cambridge, Mass.: MIT Press, 1981).

13. See Susan A. Basow, *Gender Stereotypes: Traditions and Alternatives,* 2nd ed. (Monterey, Calif.: Brooks/Cole Publishing Co., 1986), esp. ch. 2.

14. John Money and Anke A. Ehrhardt, *Man and Woman, Boy and Girl* (New York: New American Library, 1974).

15. Ibid., p. 14.

16. Beverly Wildung Harrison, *Making the Connections,* ed. by Carol S. Robb (Boston: Beacon Press, 1985), pp. 29–30.

17. These three quotations are from Matthew Fox, *Original Blessing* (Santa Fe, N.M.: Bear & Co., 1983), pp. 57–58.

18. John A. T. Robinson, *The Body: A Study in Pauline Theology* (London: SCM Press, 1952), p. 25.

19. See John S. Dunne, *Time and Myth* (Notre Dame, Ind.: University of Notre Dame Press, 1973).

20. Ibid., p. 81.

21. Maitland, *Aging,* op. cit. note 9, p. 83.

22. Ibid., p. 84.

23. I have discussed these meanings more fully in *Embodiment: An Approach to Sexuality and Christian Theology* (Minneapolis: Augsburg Publishing House, 1978) and *Between Two Gardens: Reflections on Sexuality and Religious Experience* (New York: Pilgrim Press, 1983).

CHAPTER TWO: Embracing Sexual Mystery

1. Herb Goldberg, *The New Male* (New York: William Morrow & Co., 1979), pp. 125–126, and Bernie Zilbergeld, *Male Sexuality* (Boston: Little, Brown & Co., 1978), pp. 37–69.

2. See, for example, Gerda Lerner, *The Creation of Patriarchy* (New York: Oxford University Press, 1986), ch. 2, and Rosemary Radford Ruether, *Sexism and God-Talk* (Boston: Beacon Press, 1983), ch. 2.

3. Penelope Washbourn, "My Body/My World," in Ruth Tiffany Barnhouse and Urban T. Holmes III, eds., *Male and Female: Christian Approaches to Sexuality* (New York: Seabury Press, 1976), p. 91.

4. See Eleanor L. McLaughlin, "Male and Female in Christian Tradition: Was There a Reformation in the Sixteenth Century?" in ibid., pp. 39–52.

5. See Matthew Fox, *A Spirituality Named Compassion* (Minneapolis: Winston Press, 1979), ch. 2.

6. See Carol Gilligan, *In a Different Voice: Psychological Theory and Women's Development* (Cambridge, Mass.: Harvard University Press, 1982).

7. Nancy Chodorow, *The Reproduction of Mothering: Psychoanalysis and the Sociology of Gender* (Berkeley: University of California Press, 1978), p. 170.

8. Ibid., pp. 150, 166–167.

9. Lillian B. Rubin, *Just Friends* (New York: Harper & Row, 1985), pp. 95–96. In the paragraphs that follow, I am indebted to Rubin's analysis in *Intimate Strangers* (New York: Harper & Row, 1983), ch. 5.

10. Rubin, *Intimate Strangers,* pp. 42–43.

11. Samuel Osherson, *Finding Our Fathers* (New York: Free Press, 1986), p. 125.

12. U.S. Bureau of Labor Statistics, cited in the *Minneapolis Star and Tribune,* June 6, 1987, p. 1-C.

13. See Kyle Pruett, *The Nurturing Father* (New York: Warner Books, 1987).

14. See Osherson, *Finding Our Fathers,* ch. 7.

15. Ibid., pp. 195–196.

16. See Beverly Wildung Harrison's insightful discussion in *Making the Connections,* op. cit. ch. 1, note 16, pp. 34–41.

17. Paul Tillich, *Theology of Culture* (New York: Oxford University Press, 1959), p. 10.

18. Harrison, *Making the Connections,* p. 39.

CHAPTER THREE: Embracing Friendship

1. James Kavanaugh, *Maybe If I Loved You More* (New York: E. P. Dutton Co., 1982), p. 28.

2. Quoted in Clifford P. Bendau, "Friends . . . Or Just Buddies?" *Minneapolis-St. Paul,* June 1981, p. 65.

3. See Vincent Kavaloski, "Men and the Dream of Brotherhood," in Robert A. Lewis, ed., *Men in Difficult Times* (Englewood Cliffs, N.J.: Prentice-Hall, 1981), esp. pp. 204–209.

4. Daniel J. Levinson, *The Seasons of a Man's Life* (New York: Ballantine Books, 1978), pp. 12, 335.

5. Herb Goldberg, *The Hazards of Being Male* (New York: New American Library, 1977), p. 136.

6. See Sam Keen, "Male Friendship: A Gilt-Edged Bond," *Gentlemen's Quarterly,* May 1984, p. 238.

7. Michael E. McGill, *The McGill Report on Male Intimacy* (New York: Holt, Rinehart & Winston, 1985).

8. Keen, loc. cit., p. 240.

9. See Steven Naifeh and Gregory White Smith, *Why Can't Men Open Up?* (New York: Clarkson N. Potter, 1984), p. 54.

10. L. Sprague de Camp, "Talking to Ghosts," *The New York Times Magazine,* April 7, 1985, p. 38.

11. Theodore Isaac Rubin, *Compassion and Self-Hate* (New York: Ballantine Books, 1975), p. 69.

12. See Morton Kelsey, *Caring* (New York: Paulist Press, 1981), pp. 58–66.

13. See Lillian B. Rubin, *Just Friends* (New York: Harper & Row, 1985), pp. 99–100.

14. Wilson Yates, "Men, Intimacy, and the 'Briar Patch World' of Feelings," *Nurturing News,* vol. 9, no. 1 (Spring 1987), pp. 7, 20–21.

15. Dietrich Bonhoeffer, *Prisoner for God,* ed. by Eberhard Bethge, tr. by Reginald H. Fuller (New York: Macmillan Co., 1958), p. 165.

16. Albert North Whitehead, *Adventures of Ideas* (New York: Macmillan Co., 1933), p. 277.

17. See Margaret Miles, *Fullness of Life: Historical Foundations for a New Asceticism* (Philadelphia: Westminster Press, 1981), who emphasizes the nondualistic side of early Christian ascetical practices.

18. See John Giles Milhaven, "Christian Evaluations of Sexual Pleasure," in *Annual of the Society of Christian Ethics,* vol. 17 (1976), pp. 63–74.

19. Alexander Lowen, *Pleasure: A Creative Approach to Life* (New York: Penguin Books, 1975), p. 32.

20. George Weinberg, *Society and the Healthy Homosexual* (Garden City, N.Y.: Doubleday & Co., 1972).

21. See Virginia Ramey Mollenkott, "Overcoming Sexism," in Presbyterian Church (U.S.A.), *Breaking the Silence, Overcoming the Fear* (New York: Presbyterian Church (U.S.A.)), n.d.

22. I have dealt with these issues more fully in *Embodiment,* ch. 8, and *Between Two Gardens,* ch. 7 (see ch. 1, note 23).

23. Cf. Robert Hawkins, "Homophobia: A Cultural Perspective," in Presbyterian Church (U.S.A.), *Breaking the Silence, Overcoming the Fear.*

24. See Alfred C. Kinsey et al., *Sexual Behavior in the Human Male* (Philadelphia: W. B. Saunders Co., 1948) and *Sexual Behavior in the Human Female* (Philadelphia: W. B. Saunders Co., 1953).

25. See Fred Klein, *The Bisexual Option* (New York: Arbor House, 1979).

26. Don Clark, "Homosexual Encounter in All-Male Groups," in Joseph H. Pleck and Jack Sawyer, eds., *Men and Masculinity* (Englewood Cliffs, N.J.: Prentice-Hall, 1974), p. 92.

27. Donald Evans, *Struggle and Fulfillment* (Cleveland: William Collins, Pubs., 1979), pp. 131–133.

28. Alfred North Whitehead, *Religion in the Making* (New York: Macmillan Co., 1926), pp. 16–17.

CHAPTER FOUR: Embracing Mortality

1. David E. Stannard, *The Puritan Way of Death* (New York: Oxford University Press, 1977), pp. 184–185.

2. Eugene C. Bianchi and Rosemary R. Ruether, *From Machismo to Mutuality* (New York: Paulist Press, 1976), ch. 4.

3. Quoted in Joe L. Dubbert, *A Man's Place: Masculinity in Transition* (Englewood Cliffs, N.J.: Prentice-Hall, 1979), pp. 75–76.

4. Susan A. Basow, op. cit. ch. 1, note 13, pp. 66–68, 276–284.

5. For more extended treatments of this see my book *Embodiment,* ch. 3, and Joy M. K. Bussert, *Battered Women: From a Theology of Suffering to an Ethic of Empowerment* (New York: Lutheran Church in America, 1986), ch. 1.

6. *Tertullian: Disciplinary, Moral, and Ascetical Works,* "The Apparel of Women," cited in Bussert, p. 10.

7. Augustine, *The Trinity* 12.7.10, cited in Bussert, p. 10.

8. Roger de Caen, cited in *Not in God's Image,* ed. by Julia O' Faolain and Lauro Martines (New York: Harper & Row, 1973), p. xiii.

9. Martin Luther, in a letter written to two nuns, cited in Bussert, p. 8.

10. From Susan Schechter, *Women and Male Violence* (Boston: South End Press, 1982), p. 229.

11. Bussert, *Battered Women,* p. 29.

12. James Boen, "Appeals of War: Fantasy and Brotherhood," *Nurturing News,* vol. 9, no. 1 (Spring 1987), p. 15.

13. Daniel C. Maguire, "The Feminization of God and Ethics," *Christianity and Crisis,* vol. 42, no. 4 (March 15, 1982), p. 61.

14. Stephen Howard, M.D., "The Vietnam Warrior: His Experience," *American Journal of Psychotherapy,* vol. 30, no. 1 (Jan. 1976), p. 125.

15. Sam Keen, *Faces of the Enemy* (San Francisco: Harper & Row, 1986), p. 129.

16. Ibid., p. 131.

17. Ibid., pp. 133–134.

18. See Marie Marshall Fortune, *Sexual Violence: The Unmentionable Sin* (New York: Pilgrim Press, 1983), ch. 1; Susan Brownmiller, *Against Our Will: Men, Women, and Rape* (New York: Bantam Books, 1976); and Bussert, *Battered Women.*

19. Quoted in Fortune, op. cit., p. 9.

20. See ibid., pp. 16–18. Cf. Susan Eroin-Tripp, "To Fight Acquaintance Rape on Campuses," *Minneapolis Star and Tribune,* January 1, 1987.

21. Peggy Reeves Sanday, in *Rape,* ed. by Sylvana Tomaselli and Roy Porter (New York: Basil Blackwell, 1986).

22. Alexander Lowen, *Pleasure* (New York: Penguin Books, 1975), p. 75.

23. *Handbook for Boys* (New York: Boy Scouts of America, 1934), quoted in David Cole Gordon, *Self-Love* (Baltimore: Penguin Books, 1972), p. 24. This section of the *Handbook* was not revised until 1945.

24. Lillian B. Rubin, *Intimate Strangers* (New York: Harper & Row, 1983), p. 103.

25. See James W. Prescott, "Body Pleasure and the Origins of Violence," *The Futurist,* vol. 9, no. 2 (1975), pp. 64–74.

26. Quoted in Matthew Fox, *Original Blessing,* op. cit. ch. 1, note 17, p. 287.

27. See Donald L. Berry, "Seeking a Theology of the Finite," *The Christian Century,* September 29, 1982, pp. 953–956.

28. Quoted in Matthew Fox, *A Spirituality Named Compassion* (Minneapolis: Winston Press, 1979), pp. 164–165.

29. Elizabeth Dodson Gray expresses all of this well in *Green Paradise Lost* (Wellesley, Mass.: Roundtable Press, 1981), esp. chs. 11 and 12. See also her *Patriarchy as a Conceptual Trap* (Wellesley, Mass.: Roundtable Press, 1982).

30. See Ernest Becker, *The Denial of Death* (New York: Free Press, 1973), pp. 84 and 160–162, wherein he also interprets the work of Otto Rank.

31. Joan Timmerman, *The Mardi Gras Syndrome* (New York: Crossroad, 1984), p. 74.

32. See H. Richard Niebuhr, *The Responsible Self* (New York: Harper & Row, 1963), p. 107.

33. Ibid., pp. 177–178.

CHAPTER FIVE: Embracing Masculinity

1. Mark Gerzon, *A Choice of Heroes: The Changing Faces of American Manhood* (Boston: Houghton Mifflin Co., 1982).

2. Ibid., p. 262. Emphasis mine.

3. Keith Thompson, "The Meaning of Being Male: A Conversation with Robert Bly," *L.A. Weekly,* Aug. 5–11, 1983.

4. Ibid. The original Grimm Brothers story is called "Iron Hans."

5. Cf. Madonna Kolbenschlag, *Kiss Sleeping Beauty Good-bye: Breaking the Spell of Feminine Myths and Models* (Garden City, N.Y.: Doubleday & Co., 1979).

6. I am indebted for the suggestion of Pinocchio to Harry Brod, "Why Is This 'Men's Studies' Different from All Other 'Men's Studies'?" *Journal of the National Association for Women Deans, Administrators, and Counselors,* vol. 49, no. 4 (Summer 1986), pp. 48–49.

7. Mircea Eliade, *Images and Symbols* (New York: Sheed & Ward, 1969), p. 9. Cf. Eugene Monick, *Phallos: Sacred Image of the Masculine* (Toronto: Inner City Books, 1987), p. 34.

8. H. A. Williams, *True Resurrection* (New York: Harper & Row, 1972).

9. Ibid., pp. 32–33.

10. Ibid., p. 33.

11. Ibid., p. 39.

12. Monick, *Phallos.* I acknowledge my particular indebtedness to his insights in the following paragraphs.

13. Mark Strage, *The Durable Fig Leaf* (New York: William Morrow & Co., 1980), chs. 1 and 5; also Monick, ch. 2.

14. Rudolf Otto, *The Idea of the Holy,* tr. by John W. Harvey (London: Oxford University Press, 1923). Cf. Monick, p. 26.

15. Monick calls this the "clithonic phallos"; see pp. 94–96.

16. Cf. Monick, pp. 48–49.

17. I am indebted to the Rev. Kenneth W. Taylor for these projection insights and also for pressing me to reflect more about the affirmation of genital softness.

18. See Matthew Fox, *Western Spirituality: Historical Roots, Ecumenical Routes* (Notre Dame, Ind.: Fides/Claretian, 1979); also Fox's *Original Blessing,* op. cit. ch. 1, note 17.

19. Quotations from Eckhart are taken from Fox, *Original Blessing,* pp. 132–133, 137, and 139.

20. See Robert A. Raines's beautiful meditation on sinking, in *A Faithing Oak: Meditations from the Mountain* (New York: Crossroad, 1982), pp. 9–10.

21. Rainer Maria Rilke, *Selected Poems of Rainer Maria Rilke*, tr. by Robert Bly (New York: Harper & Row, 1981), p. 21.

22. Starhawk, *Dreaming the Dark: Magic, Sex, and Politics* (Boston: Beacon Press, 1982), p. xiv.

23. See my fuller discussion of androgyny in *Embodiment* (Minneapolis: Augsburg Publishing House, 1978), pp. 98–101. While I still endorse much of that discussion, I am now inclined to move beyond the concept. A useful summary of the social-psychological literature on androgyny is found in Susan A. Basow, op. cit. ch. 1, note 13, chs. 1 and 13.

24. Nicolas Berdiaev's thought on androgyny is found mainly in his work *The Meaning of Creativeness* (1914). I am quoting the summary by Philip Sherrard in *Christianity and Eros* (London: SPCK, 1976), pp. 61–62.

25. See Karl Barth, *Church Dogmatics*, III/4 (Edinburgh: T. & T. Clark, 1961), esp. p. 166.

26. Monick, op. cit., p. 50.

27. In these reflections on power I have been particularly influenced by Bernard Loomer, "Two Kinds of Power," *Criterion*, vol. 15, no. 1 (Winter 1976).

28. Ibid., p. 14.

29. Ibid., p. 19.

30. Ibid., p. 21.

31. Bernard Loomer, "S-I-Z-E," *Criterion*, vol. 13, no. 3 (Spring 1974), p. 21.

32. See Williams, *True Resurrection*, p. 33.

33. William Phipps, *Was Jesus Married?* (New York: Harper & Row, 1970).

34. Leo Steinberg, *The Sexuality of Christ in Renaissance Art and in Modern Oblivion* (New York: Pantheon Books, 1983).

35. Ibid., p. 1.

36. Ibid., p. 17.

37. Ibid., p. 23.

38. Ibid., p. 13.

39. Patricia Wilson-Kastner's *Faith, Feminism, and the Christ* (Philadelphia: Fortress Press, 1983) is a helpful treatment of this issue.

40. The Superman image is from Tom Harpur, *For Christ's Sake* (Boston: Beacon Press, 1987), p. 32.

41. See ibid., pp. 118–119.

CHAPTER SIX: New Ways in Our Sexual Spirituality

1. *Time*, April 9, 1984.

2. Paul Ricoeur, "Wonder, Eroticism, and Enigma," in *Sexuality and Identity*, ed. by Hendrik Ruitenbeek (New York: Dell Publishing Co., 1970), pp. 13–24.

3. See "Reuniting Sexuality and Spirituality," *The Christian Century*, vol. 104, no. 6 (Feb. 25, 1987); also *Between Two Gardens* (New York: Pilgrim Press, 1983), pp. 73–80.

4. Ann and Barry Ulanov, *Primary Speech: A Psychology of Prayer* (Atlanta: John Knox Press, 1982), pp. 74–75. I am grateful to these authors for rich suggestions in their ch. 8.

5. Ibid., p. 83.

6. Nikos Kazantzakis, *Report to Greco,* tr. by P. A. Bien (New York: Simon & Schuster, 1965), p. 43.

7. Mark Gerzon, op. cit. ch. 5, note 1, p. 176.

8. Samuel Osherson, op. cit. ch. 2, note 11, p. 4.

9. Ibid., p. 196.

10. Elie Wiesel, *The Accident* (New York: Avon Books, 1970), pp. 96–99; cf. Robert McAfee Brown, op. cit. ch. 1, note 10, p. 161.

11. Osherson, p. 198.

12. Anthony Kosnick et al., *Human Sexuality: New Directions in American Catholic Thought* (New York: Paulist Press, 1977), p. 86.

13. Ibid., pp. 92–95.

14. This foundational sense of relationality is well expressed by Beverly Wildung Harrison, op. cit. ch. 1, note 16, and Carter Heyward, *Our Passion for Justice* (New York: Pilgrim Press, 1984).

15. See James E. Dittes, *The Male Predicament* (New York: Harper & Row, 1985), esp. pp. 164–165.

16. See Rosemary Radford Ruether, op. cit. ch. 2, note 2, pp. 85–92; Elizabeth Dodson Gray, op. cit. ch. 4, note 29, ch. 1.

17. Charles Birch and John B. Cobb, Jr., *The Liberation of Life* (Cambridge, Eng.: Cambridge University Press, 1981), p. 248.

18. Pierre Teilhard de Chardin, *Science and Christ* (New York: Harper & Row, 1968), pp. 12–13.

19. W. H. Auden, *Collected Poems,* ed. by Edward Mendelson (New York: Random House, 1976), pp. 285–286.